SPECTRUM

Enrichment Math

Grade 3

Frank Schaffer Publications®

Frank Schaffer Publications®

Spectrum is an imprint of Frank Schaffer Publications.

Printed in the United States of America. All rights reserved. Except as permitted under the United States Copyright Act, no part of this publication may be reproduced or distributed in any form or by any means, or stored in a database or retrieval system, without prior written permission from the publisher, unless otherwise indicated. Frank Schaffer Publications is an imprint of School Specialty Publishing. Copyright © 2009 School Specialty Publishing.

Send all inquiries to:
Frank Schaffer Publications
8720 Orion Place
Columbus, Ohio 43240-2111

Spectrum Enrichment Math—grade 3

ISBN 0-7696-5913-6

1 2 3 4 5 6 7 8 QPD 13 12 11 10 09

Table of Contents Grade 3

Chapter 1 Adding and Subtracting 1- and 2-Digit Numbers (with renaming)
Chapter 1 Pretest 1
Lessons 1–8 2–9
Chapter 1 Posttest 10

Chapter 2 Numeration through 100,000
Chapter 2 Pretest 11
Lessons 1–5 12–16
Chapter 2 Posttest 17

Chapter 3 Adding and Subtracting 2- and 3-Digit Numbers (with renaming)
Chapter 3 Pretest 18
Lessons 1–6 19–24
Chapter 3 Posttest 25

Chapter 4 Adding and Subtracting to 4 Digits (with renaming)
Chapter 4 Pretest 26
Lessons 1–6 27–32
Chapter 4 Posttest 33

Chapter 5 Multiplying through 2 Digits by 1 Digit
Chapter 5 Pretest 34
Lessons 1–5 35–39
Chapter 5 Posttest 40

Chapter 6 Division Facts through 81 ÷ 9
Chapter 6 Pretest 41
Lessons 1–5 42–46
Chapter 6 Posttest 47

Chapters 1–6 Mid-Test 48

Chapter 7 Fractions
Chapter 7 Pretest 52
Lessons 1–3 53–55
Chapter 7 Posttest 56

Chapter 8 Customary Measurement
Chapter 8 Pretest 57
Lessons 1–5 58–62
Chapter 8 Posttest 63

Table of Contents, continued

Chapter 9   Metric Measurement
Chapter 9 Pretest 64
Lessons 1–4 65–68
Chapter 9 Posttest 69

Chapter 10   Money, Time, and Calendar
Chapter 10 Pretest 70–71
Lessons 1–6 72–77
Chapter 10 Posttest 78–79

Chapter 11   Graphs and Probability
Chapter 11 Pretest 80–81
Lessons 1–4 82–85
Chapter 11 Posttest 86–87

Chapter 12   Geometry
Chapter 12 Pretest 88
Lessons 1–6 89–94
Chapter 12 Posttest 95

Chapter 13   Preparing for Algebra
Chapter 12 Pretest 96
Lessons 1–5 97–101
Chapter 12 Posttest 102

Chapters 1–13 Final Test 103

Scoring Record for Posttests, Mid-Test, and Final Test 109
Grade 3 Answers 111

Check What You Know

Adding and Subtracting 1- and 2-Digit Numbers (with renaming)

Read the problem carefully and solve. Show your work under each question.

Charlie blows up 18 balloons to decorate the house for his sister's birthday party.

1. After Charlie blows up all of the balloons, 4 of the balloons pop. How many balloons are left?

_____ balloons

2. Charlie then buys another 36 balloons. He blows these up. How many balloons are there in total?

_____ balloons

3. Charlie takes 16 of the balloons and ties them up outside. How many balloons are left to decorate the inside of the house?

_____ balloons

4. Charlie's friends Kate and Di come over with some more balloons to decorate inside the house. Kate brings 15 balloons and Di brings 17 balloons. How many balloons are there in all to decorate the inside of the house?

_____ balloons

Spectrum Enrichment Math
Grade 3

Check What You Know
Chapter 1

Lesson 1.1   Adding through 18

NAME _____

Read the problem carefully and solve. Show your work under each question.

Jorge collected bottles to recycle. On Monday, he collected 2 bottles. On Tuesday, he collected 4 bottles. On Wednesday, he collected 7 bottles. On Thursday, he collected 2 bottles.

---

1. How many bottles altogether did Jorge collect on Monday and Tuesday?

   _____ bottles

> **Helpful Hint**
>
> To find the total number of bottles collected, add together:
> 1. the total Jorge collected for Monday and Tuesday
> 2. the total Jorge collected for Wednesday and Thursday

3. Jorge wants to know how many bottles he collected from Monday to Thursday. What is the total number of bottles that Jorge collected?

   _____ bottles

2. How many bottles altogether did Jorge collect on Wednesday and Thursday?

   _____ bottles

Spectrum Enrichment Math
Grade 3

Lesson 1.2 Subtracting through 18

Read the problem carefully and solve. Show your work under each question.

In Maria's crayon collection, she has 5 red crayons, 7 green crayons, 15 blue crayons, and 3 yellow crayons.

Helpful Hint

To find the difference, subtract the **minuend** from the **subtrahend**:

minuend   12
subtrahend − 7
difference   5

1. Maria gives 1 of her red crayons away. How many red crayons does she have left?

_____ red crayons

2. Maria loses 4 of her green crayons. How many green crayons does she have left?

_____ green crayons

3. How many more blue crayons does Maria have than yellow crayons?

_____ more blue crayons

Spectrum Enrichment Math
Grade 3

Lesson 1.3 Adding 2-Digit Numbers

Read the problem carefully and solve. Show your work under each question.

Mike's collection of sports trading cards includes 32 baseball cards, 31 football cards, 65 basketball cards, and 21 hockey cards. At the store, he buys 17 more football cards and 24 more hockey cards.

Helpful Hint

To add 2-digit numbers:
1. add the ones first
2. add the tens next

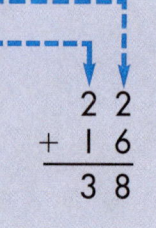

```
   2 2
 + 1 6
 ─────
   3 8
```

1. How many football cards does Mike have in all?

   _____ football cards

2. How many hockey cards does Mike have in all?

   _____ hockey cards

3. How many baseball and basketball cards altogether does Mike have?

   _____ baseball and basketball cards

Spectrum Enrichment Math
Grade 3

Lesson 1.4 Subtracting 2-Digit Numbers (no renaming)

NAME _____

Read the problem carefully and solve. Show your work under each question.

The weights of several animals at the City Zoo are shown in the table to the right.

Animal	Weight (in pounds)
chimpanzee	65
kangaroo	89
koala bear	12
raccoon	33

Helpful Hint

To find the difference between 2-digit numbers:

1. subtract the ones first
2. subtract the tens next

```
   3 6
 − 2 3
 ─────
   1 3
```

1. How much more does the chimpanzee weigh than the koala?

   _____ pounds

2. How much more does the kangaroo weigh than the raccoon?

   _____ pounds

3. What is the difference in weight between the heaviest and lightest animals in the table?

   _____ pounds

Spectrum Enrichment Math
Grade 3

Lesson 1.5 Adding 2-Digit Numbers (with renaming)

Read the problem carefully and solve. Show your work under each question.

Lauren sells raffle tickets for a charity event for the youth center. Her mother, Mrs. Jordan, buys 28 raffle tickets and her father, Mr. Jordan, buys 16 tickets. One of her neighbors, Ms. Denver, buys 17 tickets and another neighbor, Mr. Washington, buys 19 tickets.

1. How many raffle tickets altogether does Lauren sell to her parents?

    _____ tickets

Helpful Hint

To find the total number of tickets that Lauren sold, add:
1. total number of tickets sold to her parents
2. total number of tickets sold to her neighbors

3. How many total raffle tickets does Lauren sell to her parents and her neighbors?

    _____ tickets

2. How many raffle tickets altogether does Lauren sell to her neighbors, Ms. Denver and Mr. Washington?

    _____ tickets

Lesson 1.6 Subtracting 2-Digit Numbers

Read the problem carefully and solve. Show your work under each question.

Becky sells lemonade on the weekend. She buys enough lemonade to sell 80 glasses. On Saturday, she sells 34 glasses. On Sunday, she sells 18 glasses.

1. How many more glasses of lemonade does Becky sell on Saturday than on Sunday?

    _____ glasses of lemonade

Helpful Hint

To find the number of glasses of lemonade left after the weekend:
1. subtract the number of glasses sold on Saturday from the total number of glasses
2. subtract the number of glasses sold on Sunday from the number of glasses left after Saturday

3. How many glasses of lemonade does Becky have left after the weekend?

    _____ glasses of lemonade

2. After Saturday, how many glasses of lemonade does Becky have left?

    _____ glasses of lemonade

Spectrum Enrichment Math
Grade 3

Lesson 1.7   Adding Three Numbers

Read the problem carefully and solve. Show your work under each question.

Mr. Gonzalez's class is having Family Fun Night to raise money for the school. Students can win prizes by saving points from playing games. The table to the right shows what prizes students can claim and how many points are needed for each prize.

Prize	Points
balloon	10
keychain	22
ball	26
kazoo	35
yo-yo	38

Helpful Hint

To find how many points are needed to get the 3 prizes, find the prizes on the chart and add up the points listed for each prize.

1. How many points are needed to get a balloon, a keychain, and a kazoo?

    _____ points

2. How many points are needed to get a keychain, a ball, and a yo-yo?

    _____ points

3. How many points are needed to get a ball, a kazoo, and a yo-yo?

    _____ points

Spectrum Enrichment Math
Grade 3

Lesson 1.8 Addition and Subtraction Practice

Read the problem carefully and solve. Show your work under each question.

Carla has a jar of marbles. In this jar, there are 32 blue marbles and 55 red marbles.

1. What is the total number of marbles in the jar?

    _____ marbles

    Helpful Hint
    Add the number of green and purple marbles to the total you found after Carla removed the marbles from the jar.

3. After removing the 48 marbles, Carla adds 14 green marbles and 27 purple marbles to the jar. How many total marbles are in the jar now?

    _____ marbles

2. If Carla removes 48 marbles from the jar, how many marbles will be left in the jar?

    _____ marbles

Spectrum Enrichment Math
Grade 3

NAME _____

Check What You Learned

Adding and Subtracting 1- and 2-Digit Numbers (with renaming)

Read the problem carefully and solve. Show your work under each question.

Four students in Ms. Miller's class collect cans of food and bring them to school for a food drive. Chelsea collects 24 cans, Chen collects 19 cans, Ayame collects 22 cans, and Jason collects 13 cans.

1. How many cans of food altogether do Ayame and Jason collect for the food drive?

_____ cans of food

2. How many cans of food altogether do Chelsea and Chen collect for the food drive?

_____ cans of food

3. The four students collect a total of 78 cans of food. If Chelsea forgets to bring her cans of food to school, how many cans of food does Ms. Miller's class have for the food drive?

_____ cans of food

4. Three students from another class also bring cans for the food drive. Greg brings 18 cans, Carlota brings 16 cans, and Juan brings 12 cans. Altogether, how many cans do these three students bring?

_____ cans of food

Spectrum Enrichment Math
Grade 3

Check What You Learned
Chapter 1

Check What You Know

Numeration through 100,000

Read the problem carefully and solve. Show your work under each question.

The chart to the right shows how many votes each candidate received in an election for mayor. Rebecca is in charge of counting the votes and determining the winner.

Ms. Franklin	83,913
Mr. Hong	66,002
Ms. Blanco	1,084
Mr. Perez	115,014

1. Rebecca wants to write Ms. Blanco's votes in expanded form. How is 1,084 written in expanded form?

_____

2. Which person has the highest digit in the thousands place? What is the value of that digit?

_____ has the highest number.

The value is _____ .

3. Rebecca wants to compare the number of votes Ms. Franklin and Mr. Hong received. Compare the numbers by writing <, >, or = below.

83,913 _____ 66,002

4. Who won the election? What is this person's number of votes rounded to the nearest ten thousand?

_____ won the election.

_____ votes

Spectrum Enrichment Math
Grade 3

NAME _____

Lesson 2.1   Understanding Place Value (to hundreds)

Read the problem carefully and solve. Show your work under each question.

Emily is ordering beads to make necklaces. She needs 432 blue beads and 284 green beads. Beads come in boxes of 100, 10, or 1. Emily needs to find the number of hundreds, tens, and ones for each color of bead so that she can order the correct amount.

1. What is the value of 3 in 432?

   _____

> **Helpful Hint**
> Remember that the expanded form of a number is written as a sum showing the place values. For example, the expanded form of 365 is:
>
> 300 + 60 + 5

3. If Emily knows the expanded form of each number, she will know how many boxes of beads to order. What is the expanded form of each number?

   The expanded form of 432 is

   _____

   The expanded form of 284 is

   _____

2. What is the value of the hundreds digit in 284?

   _____

Spectrum Enrichment Math
Grade 3
12

Lesson 2.2 Understanding Place Value (to ten thousands)

Read the problem carefully and solve. Show your work under each question.

Steve and his friends Hannah and Manuel are playing a new board game, *Number Master*. In this game, players calculate their scores using 5 digits. The first player to 50,000 points wins.

Helpful Hint

In a 5-digit number, the place values from highest to lowest are:

1. ten thousands
2. thousands
3. hundreds
4. tens
5. ones

1. Steve has 32,914 points. What is the value of the 9 in 32,914?

   _____

2. Hannah has 43,528 points. Which digit is in the ten thousands place?

   _____

3. Manuel has 25,040 points. What is this number in expanded form?

   _____

   _____

Spectrum Enrichment Math
Grade 3

Lesson 2.3   Understanding Place Value (to hundred thousands)

Read the problem carefully and solve. Show your work under each question.

Steve, Hannah, and Manuel decide to continue playing *Number Master* but change the points needed to win to 500,000. After several rounds, Steve has 398,004 points, Hannah has 270,210 points, and Manuel has 401,035 points.

Helpful Hint

One way to find the value of a digit:
1. Cross off the numbers to the left of the digit.
2. Change the numbers to the right of the digit to 0's.

1. What is the value of the 8 in 398,004?

_____

2. Which digit is in the ten thousands place in Manuel's score?

_____

3. What is Hannah's score written in expanded form?

_____

Spectrum Enrichment Math
Grade 3

Lesson 2.3
Understanding Place Value (to hundred thousands)

Lesson 2.4 Greater Than, Less Than, or Equal To

Read the problem carefully and solve. Show your work under each question.

A group of friends started a reading club. The chart on the right shows how many pages each member of the reading club read this week.

Amy	89
Carlos	205
Chen	124
Felicia	84
Reggie	161
Tamara	210

Helpful Hint

< means *less than*
> means *greater than*
= means *equal to*

1. Who read more pages this week, Chen or Reggie? Write <, >, or = to compare the numbers.

   _____

   124 _____ 161

2. Who read more pages this week, Amy or Felicia?

   _____

3. Who read the most pages this week?

   _____

Spectrum Enrichment Math
Grade 3

Lesson 2.5 Rounding

Read the problem carefully and solve. Show your work under each question.

Carla spends the day at the city aquarium. Carla's favorite exhibits are the penguins and the jellyfish. The aquarium has 66 penguins. The jellyfish exhibit has 432 jellyfish.

Helpful Hint
If the digit you are rounding is 5 or greater, round up.

1. What is the number of penguins at the aquarium rounded to the nearest ten?

    _____

2. What is the number of jellyfish at the aquarium rounded to the nearest hundred?

    _____

3. Last month, 5,542 people visited the aquarium. What is 5,542 rounded to the nearest thousand?

    _____

Spectrum Enrichment Math
Grade 3

Lesson 2.5
Rounding

Check What You Learned

Numeration through 100,000

Read the problem carefully and solve. Show your work under each question.

Christina writes a report about her school and her city. According to a report in the local newspaper, 246,320 people live in her city. At her school, there are 345 students in her grade. Christina's older sister, Melissa, has 287 students in her grade.

1. How can Christina write the number of students in her grade in expanded form?

   _____

2. What is the value of the digit 4 in the number of people that live in Christina's city?

   _____

3. Christina wants to know if her grade or her sister's grade has more students. Write <, >, or = to compare the number of students in Christina's and Melissa's grades.

   345 _____ 287

4. Christina rounds the number of students in each grade to the nearest ten for her report. What are 345 and 287 rounded to the nearest ten?

   345 _____

   287 _____

CHAPTER 3 PRETEST

NAME _____

 Check What You Know

Adding and Subtracting 2- and 3-Digit Numbers (with renaming)

Read the problem carefully and solve. Show your work under each question.

Cindy has a collection of colorful paper clips. She has 532 yellow paper clips, 316 red paper clips, 186 green paper clips, 87 blue paper clips, and 45 purple paper clips.

1. If Cindy combines her blue and purple paper clips, how many blue and purple paper clips altogether does she have?

   _____ paper clips

2. If Cindy combines her red and green paper clips, how many red and green paper clips altogether does she have?

   _____ paper clips

3. How many more yellow paper clips than green paper clips does Cindy have?

   _____ more paper clips

4. Cindy adds the number of green paper clips to the number of blue paper clips and finds that the total is 273 paper clips. Write and solve a subtraction problem to check her answer.

   _____

Spectrum Enrichment Math
Grade 3

Check What You Know
Chapter 3

Lesson 3.1 Adding 2-Digit Numbers

Read the problem carefully and solve. Show your work under each question.

Sarah works a paper route for four weeks. The chart on the right shows how much money she earns each week.

Week	Amount Earned
1	$14
2	$22
3	$29
4	$26

Helpful Hint

When adding dollars, remember to include the dollar sign in the answer.

1. How much money does Sarah earn in total during the first 2 weeks?

   _____

2. How much money altogether does Sarah earn during weeks 3 and 4?

   _____

3. How much money does Sarah earn in total during the 4 weeks of her paper route?

   _____

Spectrum Enrichment Math
Grade 3

Lesson 3.2 Subtracting 2 Digits from 3 Digits

Read the problem carefully and solve. Show your work under each question.

Shina, Dora, and Melvin go to the store near their school. Shina has 185 pennies, Dora has 138 pennies, and Melvin has 58 pennies. The store's prices are shown on the chart to the right.

Item	Price (in pennies)
granola bar	80
banana	55
juice	125

1. Shina buys a granola bar. How many pennies does she have left after buying the granola bar?

   _____ pennies

Helpful Hint

Find the difference between the price of the juice and the number of pennies Melvin has by subtracting the smaller number from the larger number.

3. Melvin wants to buy a juice, but he does not have enough pennies. How many more pennies does he need to buy a juice?

2. Dora buys a banana. How many pennies does she have left after buying the banana?

   _____ pennies

   _____ more pennies

Spectrum Enrichment Math
Grade 3

Lesson 3.3 Adding 3-Digit Numbers

Read the problem carefully and solve. Show your work under each question.

Kenesha sells tickets to three events at her school. So far, she has sold 213 adult tickets and 226 children's tickets for a basketball game, 298 adult tickets and 315 children's tickets for the talent show, and 614 adult tickets and 438 children's tickets for the school play.

> **Helpful Hint**
>
> To add 3-digit numbers, first add the ones. Then, add the tens. Finally, add the hundreds.

1. How many total tickets has Kenesha sold for the basketball game?

   _____ tickets

2. How many total tickets has Kenesha sold for the talent show?

   _____ tickets

3. How many total tickets has Kenesha sold for the school play?

   _____ tickets

Lesson 3.4 Subtracting 3-Digit Numbers

Read the problem carefully and solve. Show your work under each question.

Roberto works at the ice cream shop. He made a chart from Monday to Friday that shows how many scoops of ice cream he sold each day.

Day	Scoops
Monday	189
Tuesday	305
Wednesday	435
Thursday	267
Friday	511

Helpful Hint

When subtracting, rename if the digit above is less than the digit below.

Example:
```
   2 15 14
   3  6  4
 - 1  8  7
 ─────────
   1  7  7
```

1. How many more scoops of ice cream did Roberto sell on Wednesday than on Tuesday?

   _____ scoops

2. How many more scoops of ice cream did Roberto sell on Friday than on Thursday?

   _____ scoops

3. On the weekend, Roberto sells 980 scoops of ice cream. How many more scoops does Roberto sell on the weekend than he did on Friday?

   _____ scoops

Spectrum Enrichment Math
Grade 3

Lesson 3.5 Thinking Subtraction for Addition

Read the problem carefully and solve. Show your work under each question.

Nick owns a furniture store. The cash register is broken, so Nick must add up the prices of furniture for customers. He also has to check his work to make sure he does not make a mistake.

Helpful Hint

Use subtraction to check an addition problem.

Example:

```
   4 0 1
 + 2 2 4
  ------
   6 2 5
 - 2 2 4
  ------
   4 0 1
```

1. Nick adds the price of a $212 chair and a $380 table to find a total of $592. Write and solve a subtraction problem to check his answer.

  _____

2. Nick solved the problem below to add together the prices of two lamps:

  ```
    $1 6 8
  + $1 3 4
   -------
    $3 0 2
  ```

  Write and solve a subtraction problem to check his answer.

  _____

3. Nick sold two desks for $165 each. He solved $165 + $165 = $320. Write and solve a subtraction problem to check his answer. Is he correct? Explain.

  _____

  _____

Spectrum Enrichment Math
Grade 3

Lesson 3.5
Thinking Subtraction for Addition

Lesson 3.6 Thinking Addition for Subtraction

Read the problem carefully and solve. Show your work under each question.

The electronics store is having a sale. The table on the right shows the original cost of several sale items and their discounts.

Item	Original Price	Discount
computer	$595	$103
camera	$208	$72
television	$462	$138

Helpful Hint

Use addition to check a subtraction problem.

Example:

```
   5 9 5
 − 3 4 4
   2 5 1
 + 3 4 4
   5 9 5
```

1. Shane wants to buy a computer. He calculates the discounted price as $492. Write and solve an addition problem to check his answer.

2. Carmen wants to buy a camera. She calculates the discounted price as $136. Write and solve an addition problem to check her answer.

3. Ella wants to buy a television. When she gets to the register, the cashier charges her $334. Solve with subtraction and check the answer using addition. Is the cashier correct? Explain.

Check What You Learned

Adding and Subtracting 2- and 3-Digit Numbers (with renaming)

Read the problem carefully and solve. Show your work under each question.

Bookworm's Bookstore sells used books. The owner of the bookstore checks the inventory and finds that the store has 564 fiction books, 412 nonfiction books, 169 poetry books, and 82 picture books.

1. How many more poetry books are there than picture books?

_____ more poetry books

2. The bookstore receives a shipment of books. In this shipment, there are 147 fiction books. How many fiction books does the store have now?

_____ fiction books

3. How many more nonfiction books are there than poetry books?

_____ more nonfiction books

4. The bookstore sells 75 nonfiction books. The owner of the bookstore calculates that there are now 337 nonfiction books. Write and solve an addition problem to check his answer.

_____

Check What You Know

Adding and Subtracting to 4 Digits (with renaming)

Read the problem carefully and solve. Show your work under each question.

Dave goes for a long walk every day after school. The chart to the right shows how far he walked in kilometers and how many minutes he walked during 3 days this week. Last week, he walked for a total of 52 kilometers and 778 minutes.

Day	Distance (kilometers)	Time (minutes)
Monday	10	162
Tuesday	15	225
Wednesday	8	118

1. How many kilometers altogether did Dave walk on Monday, Tuesday, and Wednesday?

   _____ kilometers

2. How many minutes altogether did Dave walk on Monday, Tuesday, and Wednesday?

   _____ minutes

3. If Dave ends up walking a total of 1,225 minutes for the entire week, how many more minutes will he have walked this week than last week?

   _____ more minutes

4. About how many more minutes did Dave walk on Tuesday than on Wednesday? Estimate by rounding each number to the nearest hundred.

   about _____ more minutes

Spectrum Enrichment Math
Grade 3

Check What You Know
Chapter 4

Lesson 4.1 Adding 3 or More Numbers (1 and 2 digit)

Read the problem carefully and solve. Show your work under each question.

Gregg and Seth are on the school basketball team. During the first three games this season, Gregg scored 8, 24, and 31 points. During the same three games, Seth scored 28, 34, and 26 points.

Helpful Hint

To add three 2-digit numbers, stack the numbers to set up the addition problem. Add the ones first and then add the tens.

1. How many total points did Gregg score during the first three games?

   _____ points

2. How many total points did Seth score during the first three games?

   _____ points

3. Gregg and Seth play another basketball game. In the game, Gregg scores 22 points and Seth scores 15 points. How many total points have each of them scored in four games?

   Gregg has scored _____ points.

   Seth has scored _____ points.

Spectrum Enrichment Math
Grade 3

Lesson 4.1
Adding 3 or More Numbers (1 and 2 digit)

27

Lesson 4.2   Adding 3 or More Numbers (3-digit)

NAME _____

Read the problem carefully and solve. Show your work under each question.

The following numbers of students attend four different schools in Lisa's town: 592, 652, 403, and 678. Lisa's friend Mike lives in another town. In Mike's town, there are also four schools. The following numbers of students attend schools in Mike's town: 712, 643, 558, and 566.

> **Helpful Hint**
> Add the number of students in the three other schools to find the number of students in Lisa's town that don't go to her school.

1. Lisa goes to the school with 592 students. How many students in Lisa's town go to a different school than her?

_____ students

2. Mike goes to the school with 558 students. How many students in Mike's town go to a different school than him?

_____ students

3. How many total students go to school in each town?

_____ students in Lisa's town

_____ students in Mike's town

Spectrum Enrichment Math
Grade 3

Lesson 4.3 Adding 4-Digit Numbers

Read the problem carefully and solve. Show your work under each question.

Students in the school band are selling two types of calendars. So far, they have sold 1,218 art calendars and 2,192 animal calendars. The students have made $2,436 from selling the art calendars and $3,288 from selling the animal calendars.

1. How many calendars have the students sold so far?

   _____ calendars

Helpful Hint

You can sometimes make the addition of three numbers easier by adding two of the numbers first and then adding the third number to this total.

3. The students also decide to sell magazines. If they made $2,392 from selling magazines, how much did they make in total?

   _____

2. How much money have the students made so far?

   _____

Lesson 4.4 Subtracting to 4 Digits

Read the problem carefully and solve. Show your work under each question.

The museum has a large collection of postcards. Reggie made the chart on the right to show how many postcards the museum has of several large cities.

City	Postcards
Chicago	2,942
New York	7,524
Los Angeles	5,230
Philadelphia	1,928

1. How many more postcards of New York does the museum have than postcards of Los Angeles?

   _____ postcards

Helpful Hint

Be careful to line up the numbers correctly.

Example:

$$\begin{array}{r} 3\,4\,9\,6 \\ -2\,3\,4 \\ \hline 3\,2\,6\,2 \end{array}$$

3. The museum uses 785 of their New York postcards for an exhibit. How many New York postcards do they have left?

   _____ postcards

2. How many more postcards of Chicago does the museum have than postcards of Philadelphia?

   _____ postcards

Spectrum Enrichment Math
Grade 3

Lesson 4.5   Estimating Addition

Read the problem carefully and solve. Show your work under each question.

Rosa has planned two concerts at the new concert hall. There are 82 musicians in the band and 26 singers in the chorus. Rosa sold 824 tickets for the first show and 798 tickets for the second show. The concert hall costs $1,211 to rent for a night, except on Saturdays, when it costs $1,560.

> **Helpful Hint**
>
> Round each number to the greatest place value that the numbers have in common.
>
> Example:
> ```
>   1 6 3  ------>    1 6 0
> +   4 8  ------>  +   5 0
>                     2 1 0
> ```

1. The principal wants to give every member of the band and chorus a flower at the end of the final show. About how many flowers does the principal need to buy?

   about _____ flowers

2. The school needs to print a program for every person who has bought a ticket. About how many programs does the school need?

   about _____ programs

3. The concerts are on Friday and Saturday. About how much will it cost Rosa to rent the concert hall for both of those nights?

   about _____

Lesson 4.6   Estimating Subtraction

NAME _____

Read the problem carefully and solve. Show your work under each question.

Brett is making necklaces for the school craft fair. He has 346 seashells, 1,923 small beads, and 68 large beads to make necklaces.

Helpful Hint

Round each number to the greatest place value that the numbers have in common and then subtract.

Example:

```
  1 3 5 7  ------>    1 4 0 0
-   2 3 3  ------>  -   2 0 0
                      1 2 0 0
```

1. Brett makes a necklace that has 25 large beads on it. About how many large beads does he have left after making this necklace?

   about _____ large beads

2. Brett makes a necklace that has 63 seashells on it. About how many seashells does he have left after making this necklace?

   about _____ seashells

3. Brett makes a necklace that has 147 small beads on it. About how many small beads does he have left after making this necklace?

   about _____ small beads

NAME _____

 # Check What You Learned

Adding and Subtracting to 4 Digits (with renaming)

Read the problem carefully and solve. Show your work under each question.

For a school project, Shelly is researching the year 2000, the year she was born. As part of the project, Shelly brought in several books of photos of her family and made the chart to the right, showing their ages that year. The chart also shows how many photographs of each person Shelly brought in.

Family Member	Age in 2000	Number of Photographs
Mother	31	212
Father	32	185
Brother	3	436

1. If Shelly adds up the ages of her mother, father, and brother in 2000, what is the total?

_____ years

3. Shelly forgot to put her aunt on the chart. If Shelly's aunt was born in 1968, how old was she in 2000?

_____ years old

2. What is the total number of photos of Shelly's mother, father, and brother?

_____ photos

4. About how many more photos of her brother did Shelly bring than photos of her father? Estimate the difference.

about _____ photos

Spectrum Enrichment Math
Grade 3

Check What You Learned
Chapter 4

Check What You Know

Multiplying through 2 Digits by 1 Digit

Read the problem carefully and solve. Show your work under each question.

Dwight and Juanita go to the post office to buy stamps. Stamps at the post office cost 5 cents, 27 cents, or 42 cents.

---

1. Dwight buys 3 of the 5-cent stamps. He wants to know the total cost of the stamps he bought. How can he write and solve this as an addition problem?

_____

2. Juanita buys 9 of the 5-cent stamps. How much does this cost?

_____ cents

3. The 42-cent stamps are for mailing letters. Dwight wants to buy 3 of these stamps to mail birthday cards. In cents, how much does this cost?

_____ cents

4. The 27-cent stamps are for mailing postcards. Juanita buys 4 of these stamps to mail postcards from a recent trip. In cents, how much does this cost?

_____ cents

Spectrum Enrichment Math
Grade 3

NAME _____

Lesson 5.1 Understanding Multiplication

Read the problem carefully and solve. Show your work under each question.

Dylan makes fruit baskets to give to his family. In each basket, Dylan puts in 3 pears, 5 bananas, and 6 apples.

> **Helpful Hint**
>
> When multiplying, remember that multiplication can be written and solved as an addition problem.
>
> Examples:
>
> 6×2 means the same as $6 + 6$
>
> 4×3 means the same as $4 + 4 + 4$

1. Dylan wrote down 5×2 to find out how many bananas he will need to make 2 fruit baskets. Write and solve the corresponding addition problem.

_____

2. Dylan wrote down 3×3 to find out how many pears he will need to make 3 fruit baskets. Write and solve the corresponding addition problem.

_____

3. Dylan wants to know how many apples he will need to make 3 fruit baskets. What multiplication problem should Dylan write to find the answer? Solve the problem.

_____

_____

Spectrum Enrichment Math
Grade 3

Lesson 5.1
Understanding Multiplication

Lesson 5.2 Multiplying through 5 × 9

NAME _____

Read the problem carefully and solve. Show your work under each question.

Emilio and Maria each make a photo album. Maria can fit 3 photos on each page of her album. She fills 9 pages. Emilio can fit 4 photos on each page of his album. He fills 7 pages.

Helpful Hint

To solve a multiplication word problem, you need to find:

1. the number of groups
2. the number of items in each group

1. Who has the most photos in their album, Emilio or Maria?

_____ has the most photos.

2. Maria takes all the photos from 3 pages of her album to school. How many photos does she take to school?

_____ photos

3. Emilio adds some photos to his album. He fills 2 more pages. How many photos does Emilio have in his album now?

_____ photos

Lesson 5.3 Multiplying through 9 × 9

Read the problem carefully and solve. Show your work under each question.

Kevin buys school supplies. He buys markers, pencils, and erasers.

> **Helpful Hint**
>
> Multiply the number of pencils in each package by the number of packages Kevin buys.

1. Pencils come in packages of 6. If Kevin buys 4 packages, how many pencils will he have?

   _____ pencils

2. Markers come in packages of 7. If Kevin buys 5 packages, how many markers will he have?

   _____ markers

3. Erasers come in boxes of 9. If Kevin buys 8 boxes, how many erasers will he have?

   _____ erasers

Spectrum Enrichment Math
Grade 3

Lesson 5.4 Multiplying 2 Digits by 1 Digit

NAME _____

Read the problem carefully and solve. Show your work under each question.

David shops for clothes at the local department store, which is having a sale. A pair of pants costs $42, a shirt costs $21, and a sweater costs $51.

Helpful Hint

To multiply a 2-digit number by a 1-digit number, multiply the ones, then the tens. Remember to carry the dollar sign to your answer.

Example:

$$\begin{array}{r} \$94 \\ \times2 \\ \hline \$188 \end{array}$$

2. David wants to buy 4 pairs of pants. How much does this cost?

   _____

1. David wants to buy 4 shirts. How much does this cost?

   _____

3. David wants to buy 5 sweaters. How much does this cost?

   _____

Lesson 5.5 Multiplying 2 Digits by 1 Digit (with renaming)

Read the problem carefully and solve. Show your work under each question.

Carrie works for a catering company that sells large food platters. The chart on the right shows how many people each platter can feed.

Platter	Number of Meals
Sandwich	28
Salad	37
Pasta	46

Helpful Hint

Rename the top number in a multiplication problem if needed.

Example:
$$\begin{array}{r} \overset{1}{2}\,6 \\ \times3 \\ \hline 7\,8 \end{array}$$

1. The local bank orders 2 sandwich platters. How many people can these platters feed?

   _____ people

2. The convention center orders 3 pasta platters. How many people can these platters feed?

   _____ people

3. The teachers at the elementary school order 4 salad platters. How many people can these platters feed?

   _____ people

Spectrum Enrichment Math
Grade 3

NAME _____

 # Check What You Learned

Multiplying through 2 Digits by 1 Digit

Read the problem carefully and solve. Show your work under each question.

Erin is having a yard sale. She is selling books for $3, toys for $5, and dishes for $2.

1. Lee buys 4 toys. Erin wants to find the total cost for the toys. How can she write and solve this as an addition problem?

   _____

3. Ms. Kwan lives next door to Erin. She buys 23 dishes at the yard sale. How much does this cost?

   _____

2. Erin's teacher, Mr. Garcia, buys 8 books. How much does this cost?

   _____

4. Kim works at the youth center. She buys 17 toys at the yard sale. How much does this cost?

   _____

Spectrum Enrichment Math
Grade 3

Check What You Know

Division Facts through 81 ÷ 9

Read the problem carefully and solve. Show your work under each question.

The third grade is having a science fair. Each classroom splits up into groups to work on projects. The chart on the right shows the number of students in several third-grade classes.

Teacher	Number of Students
Ms. Brady	21
Mr. Delgado	27
Mr. Sklar	25
Ms. Vega	28

1. Ms. Vega writes the problem 28 ÷ 7 = 4 to figure out how many students will be in each group if there are 7 groups. How is 28 ÷ 7 = 4 read?

   _____ divided by 7 is equal to _____ .

2. Ms. Brady's class is splitting into groups of 3 students. How many groups are there?

   _____ groups

3. Mr. Sklar decides to split his class into 5 equal groups. How many students are in each group?

   _____ students

4. Mr. Delgado splits his class into 9 equal groups. How many students are in each group?

   _____ students

Spectrum Enrichment Math
Grade 3

Check What You Know
Chapter 6

41

Lesson 6.1 Understanding Division

Read the problem carefully and solve. Show your work under each question.

Beatriz brings 20 bottles of water and 8 apples to tennis practice. There are 4 people at tennis practice.

Helpful Hint

In the equation $18 \div 3 = 6$, 3 is the **divisor**, 18 is the **dividend**, and 6 is the **quotient**.

1. Beatriz wants to divide the apples evenly among the people at tennis practice, so she writes $4\overline{)8}^{\,2}$. Complete the sentence below.

    In $4\overline{)8}^{\,2}$, the divisor is _____, the dividend is _____, and the quotient is _____.

2. Beatriz wants to divide the bottles of water evenly among the people at practice, so she writes the problem $20 \div 4 = 5$. Complete the sentence below.

    $20 \div 4 = 5$ is read "_____ divided by 4 is equal to _____."

3. The coach brings 24 tennis balls to practice. He wants to divide the balls evenly among the 4 players. Draw 24 balls below, dividing them evenly into 4 groups. How many tennis balls are in each group?

    _____ tennis balls

Spectrum Enrichment Math
Grade 3

Lesson 6.2 Dividing through 27 ÷ 3

Read the problem carefully and solve. Show your work under each question.

Joe is opening a pet store. He has 9 turtles, 14 snails, and 24 goldfish that he will put into fish tanks around the store.

Helpful Hint
Write and solve the corresponding multiplication problem to check the answer for each division problem.

1. Joe has 3 tanks for turtles. He wants to put the same number in each tank. How many turtles will he put in each tank?

   _____ turtles

2. Joe has 2 tanks for snails. He wants to put the same number of snails in each tank. How many snails will he put in each tank?

   _____ snails

3. Joe has 3 tanks for goldfish. If Joe puts the same number of goldfish in each tank, how many goldfish will be in each tank?

   _____ goldfish

Spectrum Enrichment Math
Grade 3

Lesson 6.3 Dividing through 54 ÷ 6

Read the problem carefully and solve. Show your work under each question.

The students in Cora's grade have after-school activities. Students can choose between playing trivia, running a relay race, or coloring.

Helpful Hint

To find the number of students on each team, divide the total students by the number of teams.

1. 24 students decide to play trivia. These students divide evenly into 4 teams. How many students are on each team?

   _____ students on each team

2. 20 students decide to run in the relay race. There are 4 students on each team. How many teams are there?

   _____ teams

3. Only 6 students decide to color. There are 54 crayons. If each student gets the same number of crayons, how many crayons will each student get?

   Each student will get _____ crayons.

Spectrum Enrichment Math
Grade 3
44

Lesson 6.4 Dividing through 81 ÷ 9

Read the problem carefully and solve. Show your work under each question.

Lita volunteers at the hospital. The table on the right shows how many hours she worked each month for the past 3 months.

Month	Total Hours
March	32
April	42
May	45

> **Helpful Hint**
> Remember that Lita works the same number of hours every day she volunteers in March. Divide the total hours by the number of days to find how long she worked each day.

1. In March, Lita worked the same number of hours each day that she volunteered. If she worked a total of 8 days, how many hours did she work each day?

    _____ hours

2. In April, Lita worked a total of 7 days. If she worked the same number of hours each day, how many hours did she work each day?

    _____ hours

3. In May, Lita worked a total of 9 days. If she worked the same number of hours each day, how many hours did she work each day?

    _____ hours

Spectrum Enrichment Math
Grade 3

NAME _____

Lesson 6.5   Division & Multiplication Practice

Read the problem carefully and solve. Show your work under each question.

Mieko prepares for a birthday party for her friend Beth. Mieko knows that there will be 24 people at the party. She sets up 3 tables for people to sit and eat. She also plans to give everyone 6 party favors each.

> **Helpful Hint**
> Be careful to know when to multiply or to divide to find your answer.

1. Mieko wants the same number of people to sit at each table. How many chairs should she put at each table?

   _____ chairs

2. How many party favors does Mieko need in total?

   _____ party favors

3. At the party, everyone plays a board game. There are 4 teams, and each team has the same number of people. How many people are on each team?

   _____ people

Spectrum Enrichment Math
Grade 3

46

Lesson 6.5
Division & Multiplication Practice

Check What You Learned

Division Facts through 81 ÷ 9

Read the problem carefully and solve. Show your work under each question.

On Saturday, Mr. Davis gives away stickers to students who come into his art store. He has 18 animal stickers, 27 sports stickers, 30 flower stickers, and 72 balloon stickers.

1. Mr. Davis splits up the animal stickers evenly among the first 6 students who come to his store in the morning. He writes the problem 18 ÷ 6 = 3. Complete the sentence below to show Mr. Davis's problem.

   _____ divided by 6 is equal to _____ .

2. Later in the morning, 3 players from the school baseball team come into the store. Mr. Davis divides the sports stickers evenly among them. How many stickers does each player get?

   _____ stickers

3. Around noon, 6 students who are in the school play come into the store. Mr. Davis divides the flower stickers evenly among them. How many flower stickers does each student get?

   _____ stickers

4. Mr. Davis gives away all the balloon stickers to a group of students in the afternoon. He gives 8 balloon stickers to each student. How many students are there?

   _____ students

Spectrum Enrichment Math
Grade 3

Mid-Test Chapters 1–6

Read the problem carefully and solve. Show your work under each question.

Jane is going to take a bus to her grandparents' house. She gets to the bus station early and must wait for the next bus to her grandparents' town. When she gets to the bus station, there are 81 people at the station including Jane.

1. Shortly after Jane gets to the station, 27 people leave on a bus. How many people are at the bus station now?

   _____ people

2. Three buses arrive at the station to drop off people. The three buses have the following numbers of people: 29, 36, and 9. How many total people got off the three buses?

   _____ people

3. Later, there are 67 people at the bus station. Write <, >, or = to compare this number with the 81 people who were at the station when Jane first got there.

   67 _____ 81

4. Jane's bus is finally ready to leave 126 minutes after she got to the bus station. Jane had expected to wait no more than 30 minutes. What is the difference between the number of minutes she expected to wait and the number of minutes she actually waited?

   _____ minutes

Spectrum Enrichment Math
Grade 3

Mid-Test Chapters 1–6

Read the problem carefully and solve. Show your work under each question.

Dan works at a toy factory. The toy factory makes 6,753 toys every week. Dan is in charge of shipping these toys all over the country.

---

1. How can Dan write the number 6,753 in expanded form?

_____

2. Dan rounds the number of toys to the nearest hundred to know how many boxes he will ship out each week. What is 6,753 rounded to the nearest hundred?

_____

3. Of the total number of toys that the factory makes each week, 1,389 are trains. How many of the toys are not trains?

_____ toys

4. The toy factory is going to expand so that it can make 2,418 more toys every week. After this expansion, how many toys will the factory make each week?

_____ toys

NAME _____

Mid-Test Chapters 1–6

Read the problem carefully and solve. Show your work under each question.

Asa, Juan, and Suzie are students at the elementary school. They help Ms. Hardy, the school librarian, in the library.

1. The 3 students each take 9 books from the book return and put them back on the shelves. How many books altogether did they put back on the shelves?

_____ books

2. Ms. Hardy asks Juan to put this month's new books on display. There are 6 stacks of new books that Ms. Hardy wants to put on display. There are 8 books in each stack. How many new books are there?

_____ new books

3. Suzie is going to move 4 shelves of mystery books to a different part of the library. There are 32 mystery books on each shelf. How many mystery books will Suzie move?

_____ mystery books

4. Asa is going to fill 5 empty shelves with biographies. He plans to put 17 books on each shelf. How many total biographies will Asa put on the empty shelves?

_____ biographies

Mid-Test Chapters 1–6

Read the problem carefully and solve. Show your work under each question.

Kamala plants a garden in her backyard. She plants 56 tomato plants, 30 pepper plants, 81 strawberry plants, and 24 basil plants.

---

1. Kamala plants the basil in 3 rows of her garden, planting the same number of basil plants in each row. How many basil plants are in each row?

_____ basil plants

2. Kamala plants the peppers in 5 rows of her garden, planting the same number of pepper plants in each row. How many pepper plants are in each row?

_____ pepper plants

3. Each row of tomatoes in Kamala's garden has 8 plants. How many rows of tomatoes does she have?

_____ rows of tomatoes

4. Each row of strawberries in Kamala's garden has 9 plants. How many rows of strawberry plants does she have?

_____ rows of strawberries

Check What You Know

Fractions

Read the problem carefully and solve. Show your work under each question.

Kyle helps decorate the school gym for a party. He paints banners that will hang from the wall. So far, he has painted $\frac{3}{4}$ of one banner and $\frac{2}{3}$ of another banner.

1. Draw a rectangle and shade $\frac{3}{4}$ to show how much of the first banner Kyle has painted.

2. Draw a rectangle and shade $\frac{2}{3}$ to show how much of the second banner Kyle has painted.

3. Use >, <, or = to compare the two fractions.

   $\frac{3}{4}$ _____ $\frac{2}{3}$

4. When Kyle finishes these 2 banners, he will have completed $\frac{2}{6}$ of the total number of banners that he plans to paint. Draw and shade a set of squares that shows $\frac{2}{6}$.

Spectrum Enrichment Math
Grade 3

Lesson 7.1 Parts of a Whole

Read the problem carefully and solve. Show your work under each question.

Maggie made dinner for her family. She made a pan of lasagna, a big bowl of salad, and a loaf of garlic bread.

> **Helpful Hint**
>
> In a fraction, the **numerator** is the part of the whole and the **denominator** is the parts in all.
>
> numerator - - - - → $\frac{1}{4}$
> denominator - - - -

1. Maggie's family ate $\frac{1}{2}$ of the lasagna. Draw a rectangle and shade $\frac{1}{2}$ to show how much of the lasagna they ate.

2. Maggie's family ate $\frac{3}{4}$ of the salad. Draw a square and shade $\frac{3}{4}$ to show how much of the salad they ate.

3. Maggie's family ate $\frac{5}{8}$ of the garlic bread. Draw a rectangle and shade $\frac{5}{8}$ to show how much of the garlic bread they ate.

Spectrum Enrichment Math
Grade 3

Lesson 7.2 Parts of a Set

Read the problem carefully and solve. Show your work under each question.

Natalia draws shapes for an art project. She needs to draw 2 triangles and 8 squares.

1. Natalia wants to shade $\frac{1}{2}$ of the set of triangles. Draw the total number of triangles that she needs for her project and shade $\frac{1}{2}$ of the set.

Helpful Hint

Draw each set, then find the parts shaded out of the total parts in the set.

3. Natalia adds the two groups of shapes together. What fraction of the entire group of shapes is shaded?

   _____

2. Natalia wants to shade $\frac{3}{8}$ of the set of squares. Draw the total number of squares that she needs for her project and shade $\frac{3}{8}$ of the set.

Spectrum Enrichment Math
Grade 3

Lesson 7.3   Comparing Fractions

Read the problem carefully and solve. Show your work under each question.

Lourdes and Beth are in the same classes. They are working on their homework at the library. After an hour at the library, they compare how much of their homework they each have completed.

Helpful Hint

To compare fractions, draw each fraction as a shaded figure and see which fraction has more shaded.

1. Lourdes has completed $\frac{3}{4}$ of her homework. Beth has completed $\frac{1}{2}$ of her homework. Draw and shade two squares to model the fractions $\frac{3}{4}$ and $\frac{1}{2}$.

2. Use $>$, $<$, or $=$ to compare the amount of homework each girl has completed. Who has finished a larger fraction of her homework?

   $\frac{3}{4}$ _____ $\frac{1}{2}$

   _____ has finished more homework

3. The girls' classmate Ryan joins them in the library. He says that he has completed $\frac{2}{4}$ of his homework. Use $>$, $<$, or $=$ to compare this fraction to the two girls.

   $\frac{2}{4}$ _____ $\frac{3}{4}$

   $\frac{2}{4}$ _____ $\frac{1}{2}$

Spectrum Enrichment Math
Grade 3

NAME _____

 # Check What You Learned

Fractions

Read the problem carefully and solve. Show your work under each question.

Flora and Kelly are at camp. They write postcards to family and friends back home. So far, Flora has written $\frac{4}{8}$ of a postcard to her brother. Kelly has written $\frac{1}{2}$ of a postcard to her parents.

1. Draw a rectangle and shade $\frac{4}{8}$ to show how much of the postcard Flora has written.

2. Draw a rectangle and shade $\frac{1}{2}$ to show how much of the postcard Kelly has written.

3. Use >, <, or = to compare the two fractions.

   $\frac{4}{8}$ _____ $\frac{1}{2}$

4. By the end of the day, the girls are ready to send $\frac{7}{10}$ of the number of postcards they plan to send from camp. Draw this fraction as a set.

Spectrum Enrichment Math
Grade 3

Check What You Learned
Chapter 7

56

Check What You Know

Customary Measurement

Read the problem carefully and solve. Show your work under each question.

Jackie went to her neighbor's yard sale. She bought a toy car, a pot, and a winter jacket.

1. What is the length of the toy car? Use a ruler to find the length to the nearest inch.

_____ in.

2. The pot that Jackie bought holds up to 3 quarts of water. How many cups of water can it hold?

_____ c

3. The pot weighs 5 pounds. Which weighs more, 5 pounds or 5 ounces?

_____

4. It's too warm for Jackie to wear the winter jacket she bought. The temperature outside is 68°F. If the temperature gets below 40°F, Jackie will wear the jacket. What is the difference between these two temperatures?

_____ °F

Spectrum Enrichment Math
Grade 3

Lesson 8.1   Measuring in Inches

NAME _____

Read the problem carefully and solve. Show your work under each question.

Frank cleans his room. He wants to measure several of the objects he finds in his room to the nearest inch.

> **Helpful Hint**
> To measure to the nearest inch, line your ruler up below the object. Measure the object, rounding to the closest whole number.

1. What is the length of the crayon?

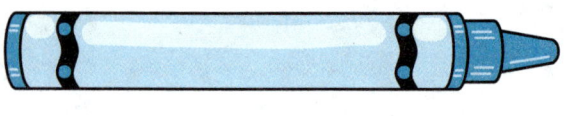

_____ in.

2. What is the length of the paper clip?

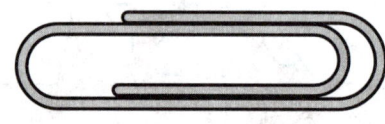

_____ in.

3. What is the length of the pencil?

_____ in.

Lesson 8.2 — Converting Units of Length (inches, feet, and yards)

Read the problem carefully and solve. Show your work under each question.

Ruth makes dresses to sell at the clothing store downtown. She needs to buy fabric to make the dresses. She will buy blue, green, and red fabric.

> **Helpful Hint**
> Use the following equalities to convert units of length:
> 1 foot (ft.) = 12 inches (in.)
> 1 yard (yd.) = 3 feet (ft.)
> 1 yard (yd.) = 36 inches (in.)

1. Ruth needs 21 feet of blue fabric. How many yards of blue fabric does she need?

   _____ yd.

2. Ruth needs 36 inches of green fabric. How many feet of green fabric does she need?

   _____ ft.

3. If Ruth has enough money left over from buying the other two fabrics, she wants to buy 9 feet of red fabric. How many inches of red fabric does she want?

   _____ in.

Lesson 8.3   Measuring Liquid Volume (cups, pints, quarts, and gallons)

Read the problem carefully and solve. Show your work under each question.

Elaine sells homemade apple cider at the farmers' market. When she fills containers of cider, she measures the cider in either quarts or gallons.

Helpful Hint

Use the following equalities to convert units of liquid volume:

1 pint (pt.) = 2 cups (c.)
1 quart (qt.) = 2 pints (pt.)
1 quart (qt.) = 4 cups (c.)
1 gallon (gal.) = 4 quarts (qt.)
1 gallon (gal.) = 8 pints (pt.)
1 gallon (gal.) = 16 cups (c.)

1. Mr. Roy wants to buy 12 cups of cider. How many quarts does he want to buy?

   _____ qt.

2. Ms. Santos wants to buy 14 pints of cider. How many quarts does she want to buy?

   _____ qt.

3. The elementary school principal, Ms. Perez, wants to bring 64 pints of cider to a meeting with parents. How many gallons does she want?

   _____ gal.

Spectrum Enrichment Math
Grade 3

Lesson 8.4   Weight (ounces and pounds)

NAME _____

Read the problem carefully and solve. Show your work under each question.

Julieta is at the supermarket for her weekly shopping trip. Some of the items on her list are sugar, flour, lettuce, and potatoes.

> **Helpful Hint**
>
> Pounds and ounces measure weight:
>
> 1 pound (lb.) = 16 ounces (oz.)
> A pencil weighs about an ounce.
> A can of food weighs about a pound.

1. Julieta buys a box of sugar that weighs 2 pounds. She also buys a bag of flour that weighs 34 ounces. Which weighs more, 2 pounds or 34 ounces?

   _____

2. Julieta buys 14 ounces of lettuce and 2 pounds of potatoes. Which weighs more, 14 ounces or 2 pounds?

   _____

3. Julieta buys herself a pack of sugarless gum as a treat. Would you use ounces or pounds to measure the weight of a pack of gum?

   _____

Lesson 8.5 Temperature

Read the problem carefully and solve. Show your work under each question.

One winter morning, Kento checks the temperature outside. He measures the temperature in degrees Fahrenheit (°F). Every hour, he draws a picture of the thermometer.

1. Kento's drawing for 9 o'clock is shown below. What was the temperature at this time?

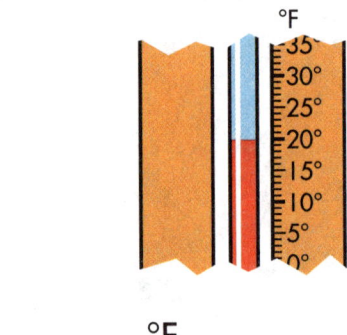

_____ °F

Helpful Hint

Water boils at 212 degrees Fahrenheit. Water freezes at 32 degrees Fahrenheit.

3. At 11 o'clock, Kento measures the temperature and finds that it is 3 degrees higher than the freezing temperature of water. Draw a picture of a thermometer that reads this temperature.

2. Kento's drawing for 10 o'clock is shown below. What was the temperature at this time?

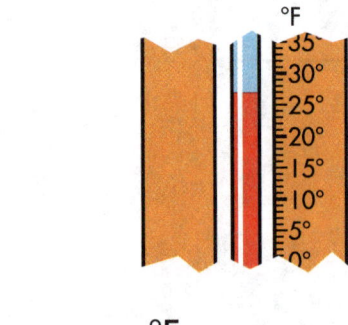

_____ °F

Spectrum Enrichment Math
Grade 3

NAME _____

 # Check What You Learned

Customary Measurement

Read the problem carefully and solve. Show your work under each question.

Deirdre buys a tropical fish and a small fish tank from Joe's Pet Store.

1. What is the length of the fish? Use a ruler to find the length to the nearest inch.

_____ in.

2. The fish tank that Jackie buys holds 10 gallons of water. How many pints of water does it hold?

_____ pt.

3. Would the empty fish tank be more likely to weigh 12 ounces or 12 pounds?

_____

4. Before Jackie can put her fish in the fish tank, the water temperature has to be 78°F. Draw a thermometer that shows this temperature.

Spectrum Enrichment Math
Grade 3

Check What You Know

Metric Measurement

Read the problem carefully and solve. Show your work under each question.

Kenesha and Roberta have a picnic at the park. They bring a basket filled with sandwiches and drinks. They also bring a blanket to sit on.

---

1. The blanket is 200 centimeters long. How long is it in meters?

   _____ m

2. Kenesha brings a 1-liter bottle of water. How many milliliters of water are in the bottle?

   _____ mL

3. Roberta wants to know how much the basket of food weighs. Should she use milligrams, grams, or kilograms to measure the weight?

   _____

4. The thermometer below shows the outside temperature in the park when Kenesha and Roberta have the picnic. Give the temperature in Celsius and in Fahrenheit to the nearest degree.

   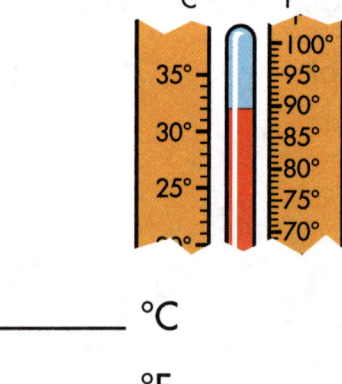

   _____ °C

   _____ °F

Lesson 9.1   Measuring in Centimeters

NAME _____

Read the problem carefully and solve. Show your work under each question.

Shawn packs his backpack for school. He measures two of the items before he puts them in the backpack. He measures to the nearest centimeter.

1. What is the length of the crayon?

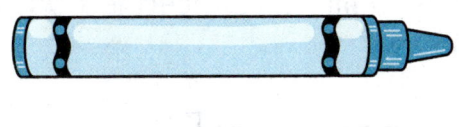

_____ cm

> **Helpful Hint**
> Meters and centimeters measure length:
> 1 meter (m) = 100 centimeters (cm)

3. Shawn rides a bicycle to school. His bicycle is 2 meters long. How many centimeters long is his bicycle?

_____ cm

2. What is the length of the eraser?

_____ cm

Spectrum Enrichment Math
Grade 3

Lesson 9.2 Measuring Liquid Volume (liters)

NAME _____

Read the problem carefully and solve. Show your work under each question.
Abby sells lemonade and iced tea at the baseball park during the summer.

Helpful Hint

Liters and milliliters measure liquid volume:

1 liter (L) = 1,000 milliliters (mL)
A single serving of juice is usually sold by the liter.

1. Abby makes the lemonade in a pitcher that holds 3,000 milliliters. How many liters of lemonade can the pitcher hold?

   _____ L

2. Abby sells 6 liters of iced tea during one hot afternoon. How many milliliters of iced tea does she sell?

   _____ mL

3. One day, Abby makes 5,273 milliliters of lemonade and 5 liters of iced tea. Which is more, 5,273 milliliters or 5 liters?

   _____

Spectrum Enrichment Math
Grade 3

Lesson 9.3 — Measuring Weight (grams and kilograms)

NAME _____

Read the problem carefully and solve. Show your work under each question.

John is weighing objects in his kitchen. He weighs a jar of peanut butter, a sugar cube, and a grain of salt.

Helpful Hint

Grams and kilograms are metric measures of weight:

1 gram (g) = 1,000 milligrams (mg)
1 kilogram (kg) = 1,000 grams (g)

1. Should John use milligrams, grams, or kilograms to measure the grain of salt?

   _____

2. The jar of peanut butter weighs 510 grams. Which is heavier, 510 grams or 5 kilograms?

   _____

3. The sugar cube weighs 4 grams. How many milligrams are equal to 4 grams?

   _____ mg

Spectrum Enrichment Math
Grade 3

Lesson 9.4 Temperature

Read the problem carefully and solve. Show your work under each question.

Kim wants to go swimming as much as possible this weekend. She measures the temperature outside each morning.

Helpful Hint
A thermometer measures temperature in degrees Fahrenheit (°F) and degrees Celsius (°C).

1. The thermometer below shows the temperature on Saturday. Give the temperature in Celsius and in Fahrenheit.

   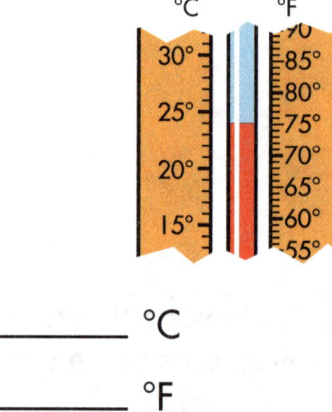

   _____ °C

   _____ °F

2. The thermometer below shows the temperature on Sunday. Give the temperature in Celsius and in Fahrenheit.

   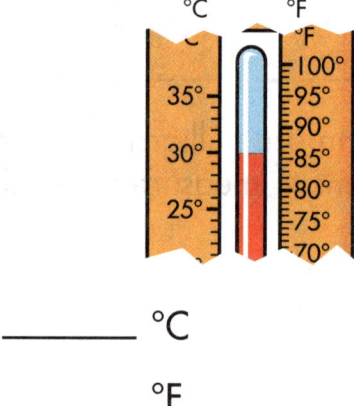

   _____ °C

   _____ °F

3. Kim will only go swimming if the temperature is above 25° Celsius. Which day or days does Kim go swimming?

   _____

Check What You Learned

Metric Measurement

Read the problem carefully and solve. Show your work under each question.

Ian wants to make spaghetti. First, he pours 2 liters of water into a large pot. Then, he puts the pot on the stove.

1. Each piece of spaghetti is 30 centimeters long. Which is longer, 30 centimeters or 3 meters?

_____

2. How many milliliters of water are in the pot?

_____ mL

3. Ian wants to know how much the pot weighs when it is filled with water. Should he use milligrams, grams, or kilograms to measure the weight?

_____

4. Ian measures the water's temperature before he puts the pot on the stove. Give the temperature in Celsius and in Fahrenheit to the nearest degree.

_____ °C

_____ °F

Spectrum Enrichment Math
Grade 3

Check What You Learned
Chapter 9

Check What You Know

Money, Time, and Calendar

Read the problem carefully and solve. Show your work under each question.

Vicki and Clarissa shop at the toy store. Vicki wants to buy a yo-yo that costs $3.78. Clarissa wants to buy a basketball that costs $7.13.

1. What is the cost of the yo-yo written as dollars and cents?

   _____ dollars _____ cents

3. What is the combined cost of both toys that the girls want to buy?

   _____

2. Vicki brought the money below to buy the yo-yo. What is the total value of this money?

   _____

4. Clarissa buys the basketball. She counts out the money shown below. How much change should Clarissa get back?

   _____

Check What You Know

Money, Time, and Calendar

Read the problem carefully and solve. Show your work under each question.

Inez is the mayor of her town. She has a very busy schedule. Today, Inez has a meeting with the school board, a ribbon-cutting ceremony at the new library, and a speech at the high school.

1. Inez meets with the school board at 10:15. Complete the sentence below.

   10:15 means _____ minutes after _____.

2. Inez goes to the library at the time shown on the digital clock below. Draw the hands on the analog clock to represent the time shown on the digital clock.

3. Inez's speech at the high school lasts for 1 hour and 50 minutes. How many minutes long is the speech?

   _____ minutes

4. Inez meets with the school board once a month. How many times does she meet with the school board in a year?

   _____

Spectrum Enrichment Math
Grade 3

NAME _____

Lesson 10.1   Money: Using Decimals

Read the problem carefully and solve. Show your work under each question.

Tim cleaned his room. As he cleaned his room, he collected any money he found and put it into a jar.

Helpful Hint
1 penny, 1 cent, 1¢, or $0.01
1 nickel, 5 cents, 5¢, or $0.05
1 dime, 10 cents, 10¢, or $0.10
1 quarter, 25 cents, 25¢, or $0.25
1 half dollar, 50 cents, 50¢, or $0.50
1 dollar, 100 cents, 100¢, or $1.00

1. Tim found 30 pennies under his bed. What is the value of 30 pennies in cents? How many nickels have the same value?

   _____ cents

   _____ nickels

2. Tim found 2 quarters in his dresser. What is the value of 2 quarters in cents? How many dimes have the same value?

   _____ cents

   _____ dimes

3. Tim found a total of $5.95 while cleaning his room. What is this amount written as dollars and cents?

   _____ dollars _____ cents

NAME _____

Lesson 10.2   Adding and Subtracting with Decimals

Read the problem carefully and solve. Show your work under each question.

Cara and her brother Sean go to the gift shop at the aquarium with their parents. The table at the right shows the prices of the items at the gift shop.

Gift Shop Price List	
Item	**Price**
toy submarine	$11.99
stuffed seal	$7.59
squirting stingray	$3.08
sea animal sticker	45¢

> **Helpful Hint**
>
> Be sure to line up the decimal points before you add or subtract:
>
> $8.52
> + $1.34
> ———
> $9.86
>
> Remember to put a decimal point (.) and a $ or ¢ in your answer.

1. Cara buys a stuffed seal and a squirting stingray. How much altogether does she spend?

   _____

2. Sean buys a toy submarine. How much more does he spend than Cara?

   _____

3. Sean also buys 2 sea animal stickers. What is the total cost of the 2 stickers?

   _____

Spectrum Enrichment Math
Grade 3

Lesson 10.3 Counting Money

Read the problem carefully and solve. Show your work under each question.

Doug works as a cashier at a supermarket. Every time a person pays for groceries, Doug counts out the correct change.

Helpful Hint

$5.00 $1.00 $0.50 or 50¢ $0.25 or 25¢ $0.10 or 10¢ $0.05 or 5¢ $0.01 or 1¢

1. Maggie buys some juice. Doug counts her change, which is shown below. What is the value of this money?

_____

3. Mr. Glenn buys a loaf of bread. Doug counts Mr. Glenn's change. His change is shown below. What is the value of this money?

_____

2. Ms. Ramirez buys a box of cereal. Doug counts her change. The change is shown below. What is the value of this money?

_____

Spectrum Enrichment Math
Grade 3

Lesson 10.4 Money: Making Change

Read the problem carefully and solve. Show your work under each question.

Shelly goes to the shopping mall to pick up a few items that she needs for school. She needs a dictionary, a pencil case, and a calculator.

Helpful Hint
To find the change, subtract the cost of the item from the value of the money given to the cashier.

1. A dictionary at the bookstore costs $3.99. Shelly counts out the money shown below. How much money will she have left over?

_____

2. A pencil case at the stationery store costs $2.25. Shelly counts out the money shown below. How much money will she have left over?

_____

3. Shelly buys a calculator for $6.82. She counts out the money shown below. How much money will Shelly have left over?

_____

Spectrum Enrichment Math
Grade 3

Lesson 10.4
Money: Making Change

75

Lesson 10.5 Telling Time

Read the problem carefully and solve. Show your work under each question.

Linda writes in a diary each day. In the diary, she writes what time she does different activities throughout the day.

1. Linda eats her breakfast at 7:50. Complete the sentence below.

   7:50 means _____ minutes

   after _____ .

3. Linda goes to the library at the time shown on the clock below. Write the time to the nearest quarter hour.

   about _____ : _____

Helpful Hint

The short hand on an analog clock shows the **hour**. The long hand on an analog clock shows the **minute**.

2. Linda goes jogging at the time shown on the clock below. Write the numerals that name the time.

   _____ : _____

Lesson 10.6 Calendar

NAME _____

Read the problem carefully and solve. Show your work under each question.

Gloria buys the calendar on the right. She wants to note certain days when there are fun activities in her hometown.

S M T W T F S	S M T W T F S	S M T W T F S	S M T W T F S
January	**February**	**March**	**April**
1 2 3 4	1	1	1 2 3 4 5
5 6 7 8 9 10 11	2 3 4 5 6 7 8	2 3 4 5 6 7 8	6 7 8 9 10 11 12
12 13 14 15 16 17 18	9 10 11 12 13 14 15	9 10 11 12 13 14 15	13 14 15 16 17 18 19
19 20 21 22 23 24 25	16 17 18 19 20 21 22	16 17 18 19 20 21 22	20 21 22 23 24 25 26
26 27 28 29 30 31	23 24 25 26 27 28	23 24 25 26 27 28 29 / 30 31	27 28 29 30
May	**June**	**July**	**August**
1 2 3	1 2 3 4 5 6 7	1 2 3 4 5	1 2
4 5 6 7 8 9 10	8 9 10 11 12 13 14	6 7 8 9 10 11 12	3 4 5 6 7 8 9
11 12 13 14 15 16 17	15 16 17 18 19 20 21	13 14 15 16 17 18 19	10 11 12 13 14 15 16
18 19 20 21 22 23 24	22 23 24 25 26 27 28	20 21 22 23 24 25 26	17 18 19 20 21 22 23
25 26 27 28 29 30 31	29 30	27 28 29 30 31	24 25 26 27 28 29 30 / 31
September	**October**	**November**	**December**
1 2 3 4 5 6	1 2 3 4	1	1 2 3 4 5 6
7 8 9 10 11 12 13	5 6 7 8 9 10 11	2 3 4 5 6 7 8	7 8 9 10 11 12 13
14 15 16 17 18 19 20	12 13 14 15 16 17 18	9 10 11 12 13 14 15	14 15 16 17 18 19 20
21 22 23 24 25 26 27	19 20 21 22 23 24 25	16 17 18 19 20 21 22	21 22 23 24 25 26 27
28 29 30	26 27 28 29 30 31	23 24 25 26 27 28 29 / 30	28 29 30 31

1. The community center has a free movie every month. How many months are there in one year?

    _____ months

> **Helpful Hint**
>
> There are 60 minutes in an hour.
> There are 24 hours in a day.

3. Gloria notes on the calendar that the annual bake sale at the elementary school lasts for 3 hours and 15 minutes. How many minutes long is the bake sale?

    _____ minutes

2. The library has a book sale every Monday in September. On the calendar, how many Mondays are in September?

    _____

Spectrum Enrichment Math
Grade 3

Check What You Learned

Money, Time, and Calendar

Read the problem carefully and solve. Show your work under each question.

Robert and Joan shop at the supermarket. Robert wants to buy bread, peanut butter, and jam so that he can make sandwiches for his school lunches this week. Joan wants to buy a box of spaghetti and a jar of tomato sauce for her dinner tonight.

Bread	$2.65
Peanut Butter	$1.94
Strawberry Jam	$4.19
Spaghetti	$0.89
Tomato Sauce	$2.98

1. What is the cost of the tomato sauce written as dollars and cents?

   _____ dollars _____ cents

2. What is the combined cost of all 3 items of food that Robert wants to buy?

   _____

3. Robert brought the money below to buy his groceries. What is the value of this money?

   _____

4. Joan's groceries cost a total of $3.87. She brought the money shown below to buy her groceries. How much money will she have left over?

   _____

Spectrum Enrichment Math
Grade 3

Check What You Learned

Money, Time, and Calendar

Read the problem carefully and solve. Show your work under each question.

The elementary school has an annual talent show. Some of the students from the elementary school will perform for a large audience in the school's gymnasium.

1. The talent show begins at 6:50. Complete the sentence below.

   6:50 means _____ minutes

   after _____ .

2. Lisa goes onstage at the time shown on the digital clock below to play a song on her violin. Draw hands on the analog clock to show this time.

3. Manuel performs a juggling act at the talent show. He has been practicing his act for 1 week. How many days are in a week?

   _____ days

4. The talent show lasts for 2 hours and 12 minutes. How many minutes long is the talent show?

   _____ minutes

Spectrum Enrichment Math
Grade 3

Check What You Learned
Chapter 10

Check What You Know

Graphs and Probability

Read the problem carefully and solve. Show your work under each question.

Ritchie asked students in his grade what their favorite colors are. He made a bar graph that shows how many students picked each color.

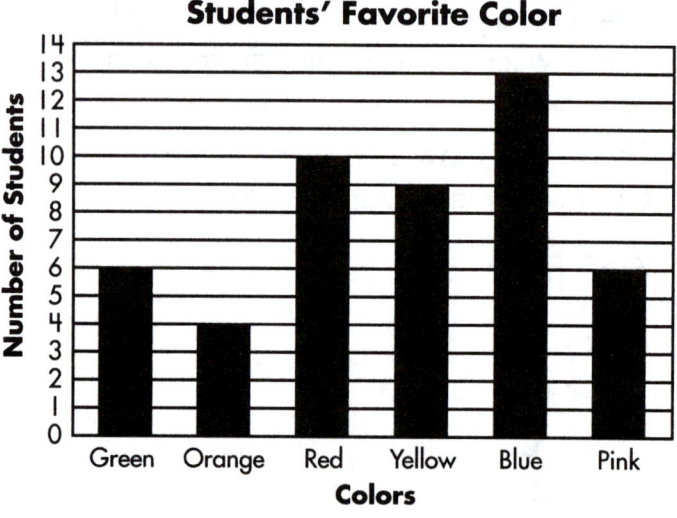

1. How many students chose pink as their favorite color?

   _____ students

2. How many students chose either green or orange as their favorite color?

   _____

3. One of the students didn't know which color to choose, so he flipped a coin to help him decide. What is the probability of the coin landing on heads?

   _____

4. Ritchie will randomly choose a completed survey. The probability of this survey being a student who chose green or pink is $\frac{1}{4}$. Indicate whether this probability outcome is "impossible," "unlikely," "equally likely," "likely," or "certain."

   _____

Check What You Know

Graphs and Probability

Read the problem carefully and solve. Show your work under each question.

Hannah studies weather in her science class. She made the line graph on the right to show the rainfall in her town over the last 6 months.

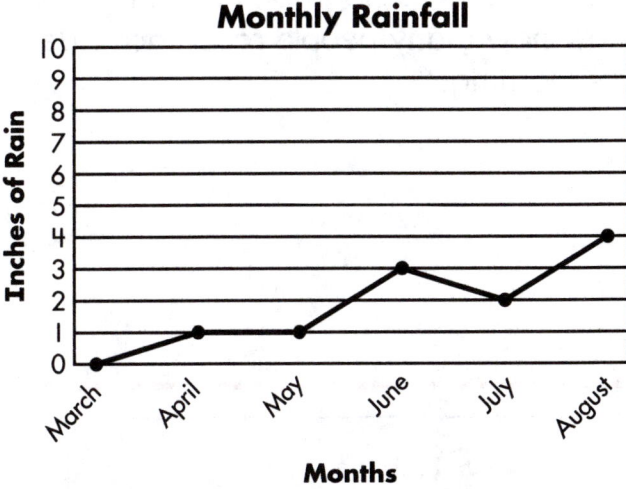

1. How many inches did it rain in June?

   _____ inches

2. In which month did it rain 2 inches?

   _____

3. How many inches altogether did it rain from March to August?

   _____ inches

4. The local weather forecaster predicts that there is a $\frac{7}{10}$ chance of rain. Indicate whether this probability outcome is "impossible," "unlikely," "equally likely," "likely," or "certain."

   _____

Lesson 11.1 Reading Picture Graphs

Read the problem carefully and solve. Show your work under each question.

Danielle works at an amusement park. She made the pictograph on the right to show how many people rode each ride this morning.

Popular Rides

Roller Coaster	웃 웃 웃 웃 웃 웃 웃
Ferris Wheel	웃 웃 웃 웃 웃
Bumper Cars	웃 웃 웃 웃 웃 ʃ
Fun House	웃 ʃ

Key: 웃 = 2 people

Helpful Hint
The **key** tells you how much each symbol on the pictograph is worth. If a stick figure is worth 2 people, a half stick figure is worth 1 person.

1. Look at the pictograph Danielle made. Which ride did the most people ride this morning?

   _____

2. How many people rode the bumper cars this morning?

   _____

3. How many people rode on the Ferris wheel this morning?

   _____

Spectrum Enrichment Math
Grade 3

Lesson 11.2 Reading Bar Graphs

Read the problem carefully and solve. Show your work under each question.

Four students run for class president in Aaron's grade. Aaron made the bar graph on the right to show how many votes each of the four students received during the class election.

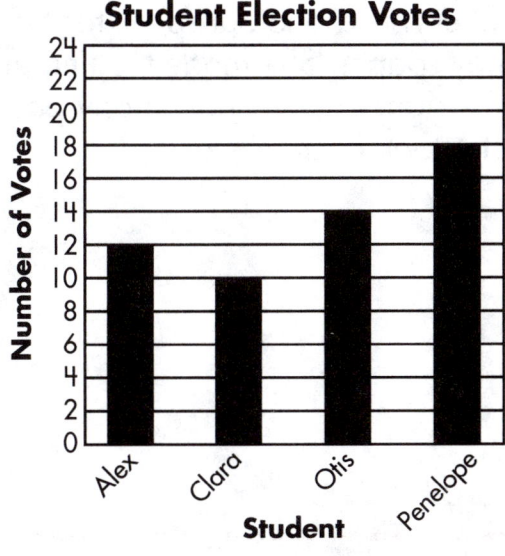

Helpful Hint

A **bar graph** shows data by representing values using a rectangle. The scale helps you find the value of each bar.

1. Which student received the most votes in the election?

_____

2. How many students voted for Alex?

_____

3. What is the difference in number of votes between the student who received the most votes and the student who received the least number of votes?

_____

Spectrum Enrichment Math
Grade 3

Lesson 11.3 Line Graphs

Read the problem carefully and solve. Show your work under each question.

Cheryl is a photographer for the local newspaper. She made the line graph on the right to show how many photographs she took each week.

Cheryl's Photographs Each Week

> **Helpful Hint**
>
> A **line graph** shows data over a period of time. Each point shows the data value at a point in time.

1. During which week did Cheryl take the most photographs?

   _____

2. How many photographs did Cheryl take in week 3?

   _____

3. During which week did Cheryl take 70 photographs?

   _____

Lesson 11.4   Probability

Read the problem carefully and solve. Show your work under each question.

Dan and Nova play a board game. To play the game, they take turns rolling a 6-sided number cube and move their piece that many spaces on the board. Dan and Nova want to know if each outcome from rolling the number cube is impossible, unlikely, equally likely, likely, or certain.

> **Helpful Hint**
>
> If the probability is 0, the outcome is **impossible**.
>
> If the probability is between 0 and $\frac{1}{2}$, the outcome is **unlikely**.
>
> If the probability is $\frac{1}{2}$, the outcome is **equally likely**.
>
> If the probability is between $\frac{1}{2}$ and 1, the outcome is **likely**.
>
> If the probability is 1, the outcome is **certain**.

1. Nova wants to roll an even number. How likely is this outcome?

   _____

2. Dan needs to roll an 8 to land on a green square. How likely is this outcome?

   _____

3. If Nova rolls a 1 or 2, she will win the game. How likely is this outcome?

   _____

Spectrum Enrichment Math
Grade 3

Check What You Learned

Graphs and Probability

Read the problem carefully and solve. Show your work under each question.

Ms. Jenkins wants to keep track of her students' birthdays, so she organizes the birthdays by season. She makes the bar graph to the right.

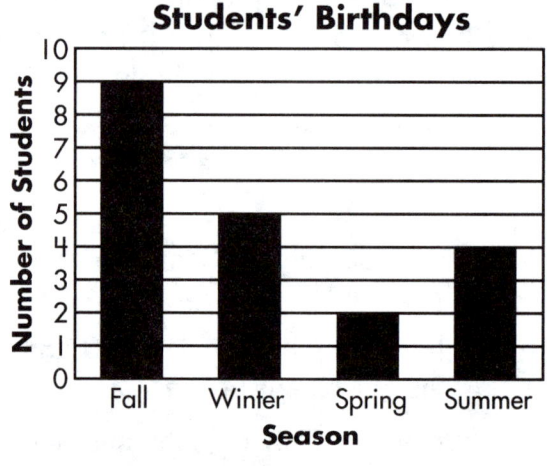

1. How many students have birthdays during the summer?

   _____ students

2. In which season do the greatest number of students have their birthday?

   _____

3. Jeff's birthday is in the winter. If Ms. Jenkins randomly chooses one of the students with a winter birthday, what is the probability that the student will be Jeff?

   _____

4. Ms. Jenkins randomly chooses another student. The probability that this student's birthday is in the fall or winter is $\frac{14}{20}$. Indicate whether the probability outcome is impossible, unlikely, equally likely, likely, or certain.

   _____

NAME _____

 # Check What You Learned

Graphs and Probability

Read the problem carefully and solve. Show your work under each question.

Matt plays on the school basketball team. He made the line graph to the right to show the number of points he scored during the first 5 games this season.

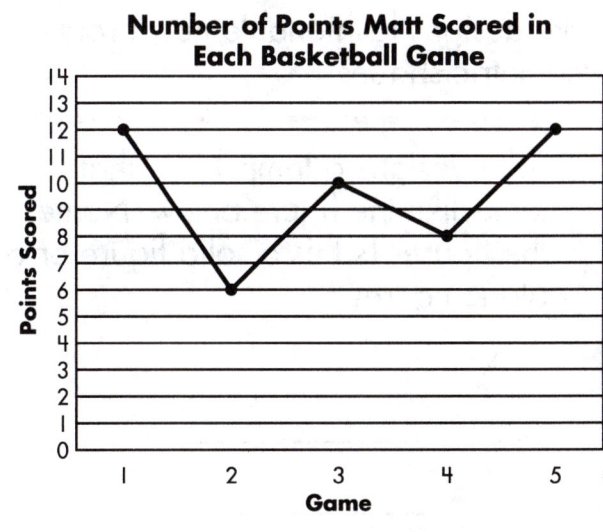

1. How many points did Matt score in game 3?

   _____ points

2. During which game did Matt score 8 points?

   _____

3. How many points altogether did Matt score in the 5 games?

   _____ points

4. There are 10 players on the basketball team. Five of those players start each game. The probability of a player being a starter is $\frac{5}{10}$. Indicate whether the probability outcome is impossible, unlikely, equally likely, likely, or certain.

   _____

Spectrum Enrichment Math
Grade 3

Check What You Learned
Chapter 11

87

Check What You Know

Geometry

Read the problem carefully and solve. Show your work under each question.

Jake designs fashionable new products for a home store. He gets his inspiration from geometric shapes.

1. Jake designs a lampshade that looks like the figure below. Name the figure. Is this a solid figure or a plane figure?

   _____

   _____

2. Jake designs 2 picture frames that look like the figures below. Indicate if these figures are congruent or not congruent.

   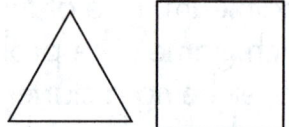

   _____

3. Jake designs a blanket that has a butterfly pattern. One of the butterflies is shown below. Indicate if the butterfly is symmetrical or not symmetrical. If it is symmetrical, draw the line of symmetry.

   _____

4. Jake designs curtains with a pattern of rays, lines, and points. What is the figure below?

   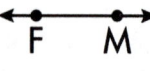

   _____

Lesson 12.1 Plane Figures

Read the problem carefully and solve. Show your work under each question.

Mr. Vaughn has students draw shapes on construction paper. Then, he has his students cut the shapes out.

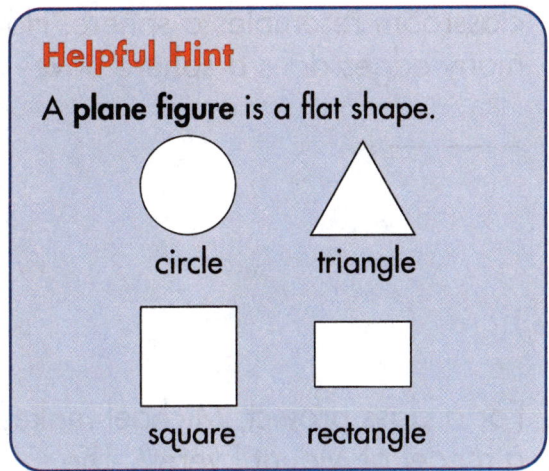

2. Mr. Vaughn has his students draw the plane figure shown below. How many sides does the figure have?

1. Mr. Vaughn asks his students to draw squares. Draw a square below.

3. Mr. Vaughn also asks his students draw the plane figure shown below. How many square corners does the figure have?

Lesson 12.2 Solid Figures

Read the problem carefully and solve. Show your work under each question.

In Michael's social studies class, they study Earth and its famous landmarks.

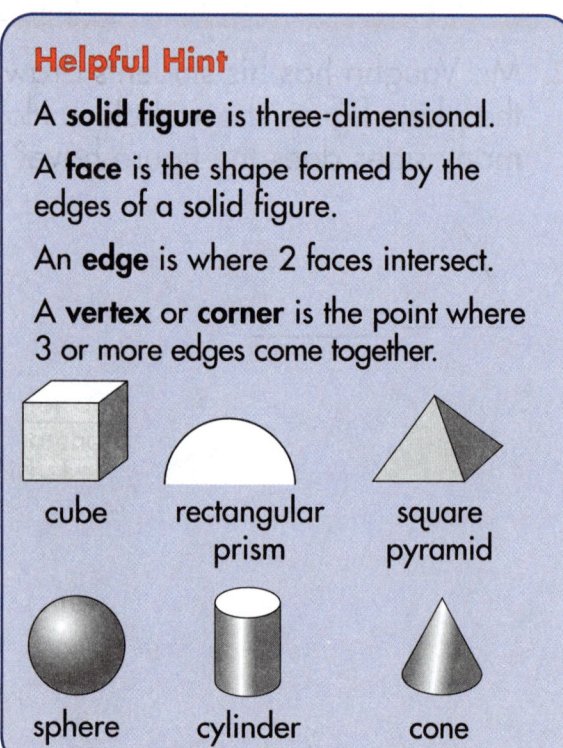

Helpful Hint

A **solid figure** is three-dimensional.

A **face** is the shape formed by the edges of a solid figure.

An **edge** is where 2 faces intersect.

A **vertex** or **corner** is the point where 3 or more edges come together.

cube   rectangular prism   square pyramid
sphere   cylinder   cone

1. The Great Pyramid in Egypt is shaped like a square pyramid. How many triangle faces does a square pyramid have?

_____

2. A globe of Earth in Michael's classroom resembles a sphere. How many edges does a sphere have?

_____

3. For a class project, Michael makes a model of Mount Everest. The model is shaped like a cone. How many square faces does a cone have?

_____

4. Michael plans to draw a map. He reaches into his pencil box for a pencil. His pencil box is shaped like a rectangular prism. How many corners does a rectangular prism have?

_____

Lesson 12.3 Comparing Figures

Read the problem carefully and solve. Show your work under each question.

Serena has a dinner party. Before the party, Serena sets the dinner table for her guests.

1. Serena puts a salt shaker on the table. The salt shaker is shaped like the figure below. Is this a plane figure or a solid figure?

Helpful Hint

Look at the faces of the solid figure to see which plane figure shape makes up most of the solid.

Example: Most of a pyramid's faces are triangles.

3. Serena buys a cake for dessert. The cake is shaped like the solid figure shown below. Draw a plane figure that is shaped like the faces of the solid figure.

   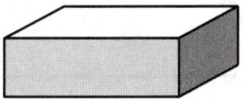

2. Serena puts a dish at each place setting on the table. Each dish is shaped like the figure below. Is this a plane figure or a solid figure?

Lesson 12.4 Congruent Shapes

Read the problem carefully and solve. Show your work under each question.

Kendra makes earrings and sells them at a jewelry store downtown. Each earring in a pair must have a congruent shape or most people won't want to buy them.

Helpful Hint

When two figures are **congruent**, they have exactly the same shape and size.

1. Kendra makes a pair of earrings using the shapes shown below. Indicate if these figures are congruent or not congruent.

   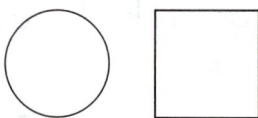

   _____

2. Kendra makes a pair of earrings using the shapes shown below. Indicate if these figures are congruent or not congruent.

   _____

3. Kendra uses the figure shown below to make another pair of earrings. Draw a congruent figure next to Kendra's figure.

   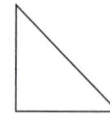

Spectrum Enrichment Math
Grade 3

Lesson 12.5 Symmetrical Shapes

Read the problem carefully and solve. Show your work under each question.

In art class, Christie cuts out some large letters from construction paper. She then covers one side of each letter in glitter. Christie has to be careful carrying these letters home in her backpack because she does not want glitter to get everywhere. She decides to fold each letter in half along a line of symmetry.

Helpful Hint

A figure or shape is **symmetrical** if one-half of the figure is congruent to the other half.

A **line of symmetry** shows the division between two congruent halves of a symmetrical shape.

Example: The letter A is symmetrical, with 1 line of symmetry

1. Christie folds the letter C along the line drawn below. Is this a line of symmetry?

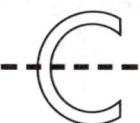

_____

2. Christie wants to give Denise the letter D. She folds the letter D along the line drawn below. Is this a line of symmetry?

_____

3. Christie wants to give Henry the letter H. Label the letter below as symmetrical or not symmetrical. If it is symmetrical, draw the line (or lines) of symmetry.

4. Christie plans to give Gina the letter G. She folds the letter G along the line drawn below. Is this a line of symmetry?

Spectrum Enrichment Math
Grade 3

Lesson 12.6 Line Segments

Read the problem carefully and solve. Show your work under each question.

Craig draws a map of his neighborhood on a piece of graph paper. He marks all of the important locations on the map using letters.

Helpful Hint

The following are examples of how to name **points**, **lines**, **line segments**, and **rays**:

point A	A
line CD	$\overleftrightarrow{CD}$
line segment XY	$\overline{XY}$
ray FG	$\overrightarrow{FG}$

1. Craig draws the route between his house, A, and the school, B. The figure below shows how he drew this route. Is this figure a point, line, line segment, ray, or an angle? Name the figure.

_____

_____

2. Craig draws the route between the library, R, and his grandparents' house, S. The figure below shows how he drew this route. Is this figure a point, line, line segment, ray, or an angle? Name the figure.

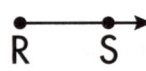

_____

_____

3. Craig labels 3 of his friends' houses as W, X, and Y. Then, he connects the houses to make the angle below. Which point is the vertex?

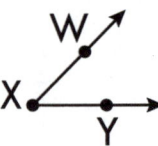

_____

Spectrum Enrichment Math
Grade 3

Check What You Learned

Geometry

Read the problem carefully and solve. Show your work under each question.

Two members of Paul's family have their birthdays next month: Paul's mother and his younger brother. Paul makes birthday cards for his mother and brother.

---

1. Paul begins by cutting a piece of paper into the shape of the figure shown below. Name the figure. Is this a solid figure or a plane figure?

☐ _____

_____

3. Paul will fold each card in half. He draws a line through the figure shown below. Is the line Paul drew a line of symmetry?

_____

2. Paul wants both birthday cards to be congruent. Indicate if the figures shown below are congruent or not congruent.

_____

4. As part of the design of the card for his brother, Paul draws a line segment on the front of the card. Draw a line segment below.

Check What You Know

Preparing for Algebra

Read the problem carefully and solve. Show your work under each question.

Brad and Jorge challenge each other to a game. They create a pattern and show the first few terms of the pattern. Then, they complete the other's pattern.

1. Brad wrote the number pattern below. Complete the pattern below using addition or subtraction.

30 26 22 _____ _____ _____

2. Brad wrote 5 number patterns and 7 geometric patterns. Jorge wrote 7 number patterns. They both wrote the same total number of patterns. Complete the number sentence below to show the number of geometric patterns Jorge made.

5 + 7 = 7 + ☐

3. Jorge wrote the geometric pattern below. Write the number of circles under each group in the pattern.

4. Brad created the geometric pattern below. Complete the pattern.

 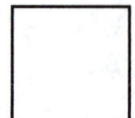 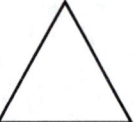 _____ _____ _____

Lesson 13.1 Patterns

NAME _____

Read the problem carefully and solve. Show your work under each question.

Laura drew patterns using objects she found around her house. She drew flowers, balls, and hats to make different patterns.

Helpful Hint
To continue a pattern, look at how each picture changes from one to the next. Look for any repetition in the change.

1. Laura drew the 3 flowers shown below. Continue the pattern by drawing the next flower.

2. Laura drew the balls shown below. Continue the pattern by drawing the next ball.

3. Laura drew the hats shown below. Continue the pattern by drawing the next hat.

Lesson 13.2 Transferring Patterns

Read the problem carefully and solve. Show your work under each question.

Bonnie organizes groups of objects. She cuts shapes from colored paper and then uses these shapes to make patterns. She makes patterns of triangles, squares, and circles.

> **Helpful Hint**
> Groups of objects can be transferred to numbers to more easily see patterns.

1. Write the number of triangles under each group in the pattern shown below.

   _____   _____   _____   _____   _____

2. Write the number of circles under each group in the pattern shown below.

   _____   _____   _____   _____   _____

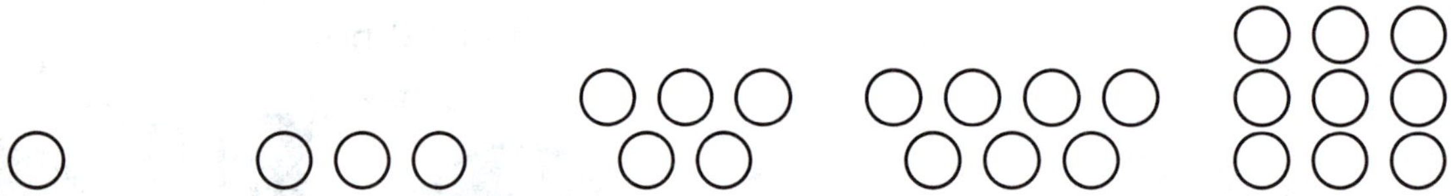

3. Write the number of squares under each group in the pattern shown below.

   _____   _____   _____   _____   _____

Spectrum Enrichment Math
Grade 3

Lesson 13.2
Transferring Patterns

Lesson 13.3 Number Patterns

Read the problem carefully and solve. Show your work under each question.

Victor started a few number patterns for his math homework. He had created half of each number pattern before dinner. Now, he can't remember how he was going to finish each pattern.

Helpful Hint
A number pattern can be created using addition or subtraction.

$25 - 5 = 20$ $20 - 5 = 15$ $15 - 5 = 10$ $10 - 5 = 5$

25   20   15   10   5

1. Use addition to complete Victor's pattern shown below.

1   3   5   _____   _____   _____

2. Use subtraction to complete Victor's pattern shown below.

16   13   10   _____   _____   _____

3. Complete Victor's pattern shown below.

7   11   15   _____   _____   _____

Spectrum Enrichment Math
Grade 3

Lesson 13.4   Geometric Patterns

NAME _____

Read the problem carefully and solve. Show your work under each question.

The students in Ms. Drake's math class are making banners that show geometric patterns. They will hang the banners on the classroom walls.

> **Helpful Hint**
> To complete each pattern, identify the repeating part of the pattern. If there is no repetition, repeat the entire group to make the pattern.

1. Phil starts the pattern shown below. Complete the pattern.

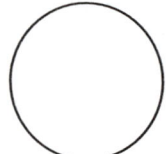  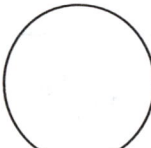 _____ _____ _____

2. Bob starts the pattern shown below. Complete the pattern.

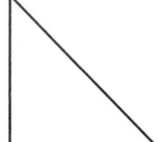 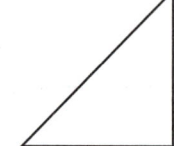 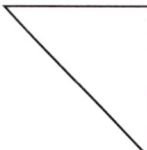 

3. Callie starts the pattern shown below. Complete the pattern.

 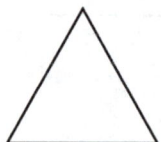  _____ _____ _____

Spectrum Enrichment Math
Grade 3

Lesson 13.5 Number Sentences

Read the problem carefully and solve. Show your work under each question.

Mr. Glenn splits his students into pairs. Each pair of students has to count the number of crayons they brought to class. Next, they will write a number sentence that compares the number of crayons they each brought to class.

Helpful Hint

Identity Property
for addition: $0 + 5 = 5$
for multiplication: $1 \times 5 = 5$

Commutative Property
for addition: $4 + 6 = 6 + 4$
for multiplication: $4 \times 6 = 6 \times 4$

---

1. Maria brought 4 crayons to class. Fred brought 2 crayons to class. They trade their crayons. Maria now has 2 crayons. Complete the number sentence to show how many crayons Fred has now.

   $4 + 2 = 2 + \boxed{}$

2. Gregg brought 6 crayons to class. Mike brought 0 crayons to class. Complete the number sentence to find out how many total crayons they have.

   $6 + 0 = \boxed{}$

3. Helen organized her crayons into 3 groups of 7 crayons. She then organized her crayons into 7 equal groups. Complete the number sentence to find out how many crayons are in each of the 7 groups.

   $3 \times 7 = 7 \times \boxed{}$

Spectrum Enrichment Math
Grade 3

NAME _____

Check What You Learned

Preparing for Algebra

Read the problem carefully and solve. Show your work under each question.

Ian makes a puzzle book to give to his friends. One section of the puzzle book has patterns to complete.

1. Ian wrote the number pattern shown below. Use addition or subtraction to complete the pattern.

   33 35 37 ____ ____ ____

2. Ian wrote 4 pages of patterns with 5 patterns on each page. He decides he wants to fit the same number of patterns onto 5 pages instead. Complete the number sentence below to find out how many patterns he should put on each page.

   $4 \times 5 = 5 \times \boxed{}$

3. Ian creates the geometric pattern shown below. Write the number of squares under each group in the pattern.

   ____ ____ ____ ____ ____

4. Ian creates the following geometric pattern. Complete the pattern.

    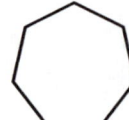   ____ ____

Spectrum Enrichment Math
Grade 3

Final Test: Chapters 1–13

Read the problem carefully and solve. Show your work under each question.

Dominic ordered 2 pizzas, a large salad, and 5 bottles of juice for a party with his friends. One of the pizzas is plain cheese, and the other is vegetable. Four of the bottles of juice are apple, and 1 is cranberry.

1. Dominic and his friends eat $\frac{5}{8}$ of the salad. Draw a rectangle and shade it to model the fraction of the salad they ate.

2. Draw a set of triangles and shade $\frac{4}{5}$ of the set to show the number of bottles of juice that are apple.

3. Dominic and his friends eat $\frac{7}{10}$ of the vegetable pizza and $\frac{3}{5}$ of the cheese pizza. Use >, <, or = to compare the fractions.

   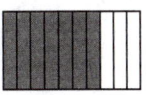 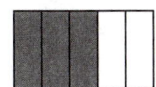

   $\frac{7}{10}$ _____ $\frac{3}{5}$

4. Dominic and his friends drink a total of 4 pints of juice. How many quarts of juice do they drink?

   _____ quarts

Final Test: Chapters 1–13

Read the problem carefully and solve. Show your work under each question.

Every school day, Lisa packs her lunch, grabs her backpack, and waits for the bus at the end of her driveway.

---

1. Is Lisa's backpack more likely to weigh 3 ounces or 3 pounds?

_____

2. Lisa packs a bottle of water in her lunch. The bottle contains 1 liter of water. How many milliliters of water are in the bottle?

_____ mL

3. As Lisa left her house, she read the outside thermometer. What is the temperature on the thermometer in degrees Celsius and degrees Fahrenheit?

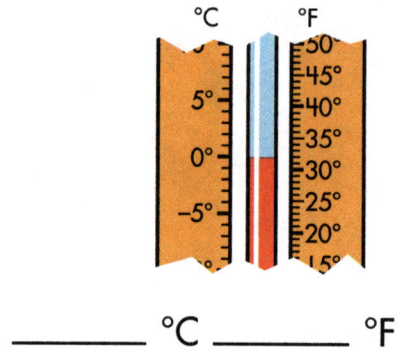

_____ °C _____ °F

4. Lisa's driveway is 4 yards long. How many feet long is Lisa's driveway?

_____ ft.

Final Test   Chapters 1–13

Read the problem carefully and solve. Show your work under each question.

Frank walked to the bookstore to buy a book for his mother's birthday. He spent 2 hours and 15 minutes looking through the books before he chose one. The book cost $8.99.

1. The time when Frank left to go to the bookstore is shown on the digital clock below. Draw the hands on the analog clock to express the same time.

3. Complete the sentence below to show what the price of the book means.

$8.99 means _____ dollars and _____ cents.

4. Frank brought the money below to pay for the book. Determine the amount of money he will have left over after he buys the book.

money brought $ _____

cost of book   − $ _____

money left over $ _____

2. How many minutes did Frank spend at the bookstore?

_____ minutes

Spectrum Enrichment Math
Grade 3

Final Test
Chapters 1–13
105

Final Test — Chapters 1–13

Read the problem carefully and solve. Show your work under each question.

Nina asked the students in her grade what their favorite pets are. Nina used the results of her survey to make the bar graph to the right.

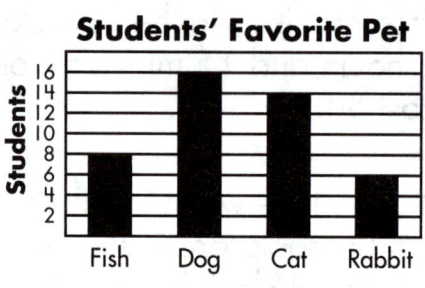

1. Which animal did 14 students choose as their favorite pet?

   _____

2. How many students chose either dog or cat as their favorite pet?

   _____ students

3. If Nina randomly picked one of the categories, she has $\frac{1}{4}$ chance of picking fish. Is this probability impossible, unlikely, equally likely, likely, or certain?

   _____

4. Nina interviewed 44 students for her survey. She wants to interview 3 times that many students for her next survey. Multiply to find how many students she wants to survey next time.

   $$\begin{array}{r} 44 \\ \times\ 3 \\ \hline \end{array}$$

   _____

Spectrum Enrichment Math
Grade 3

Final Test: Chapters 1–13

Read the problem carefully and solve. Show your work under each question.

Jennifer helps her parents clean the garage for a yard sale. She packs items that her parents plan to sell into boxes. Then, she labels each box.

1. Each box looks like the cube shown below. How many square faces does a cube have?

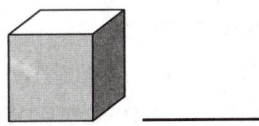

2. Jennifer packs a ball into one of the boxes. The ball is shaped like the figure shown below. Is this a plane figure or a solid figure?

3. Jennifer labels one of the boxes by drawing the two figures shown below on the top of the box. Are these figures congruent or not congruent?

4. Jennifer draws the letter shown below on one of the boxes. Label the letter as symmetrical or not symmetrical. If the letter is symmetrical, draw the line (or lines) of symmetry.

Final Test: Chapters 1–13

Read the problem carefully and solve. Show your work under each question.

Austin draws patterns on construction paper for a craft project. He starts by drawing the pattern shown below.

1. Write the number of triangles from left to right in each group of Austin's pattern.

   _____ _____ _____

   _____ _____

2. Austin extends his pattern by adding three more groups of triangles. Using addition, find how many triangles will be in each of the next three groups.

   _____ _____ _____

3. Austin draws 2 patterns on each page of 6 pieces of construction paper. If he wants to draw the same total number of patterns on 4 pages, how many patterns does he need to draw on each page? Complete the number sentence below to solve.

   $6 \times 2 = 4 \times \square$

4. Austin starts a repeating pattern by drawing the three shapes shown below. Draw the next three shapes to continue his pattern.

   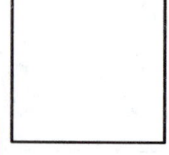 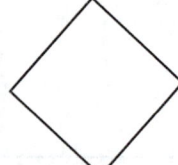 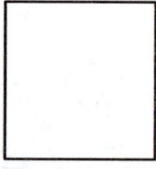   _____ _____ _____

NAME _____   DATE _____

Scoring Record for Posttests, Mid-Test, and Final Test

Chapter Posttest	Your Score	Performance			
		Excellent	Very Good	Fair	Needs Improvement
1	___ of 4	4	3	2	1
2	___ of 4	4	3	2	1
3	___ of 4	4	3	2	1
4	___ of 4	4	3	2	1
5	___ of 4	4	3	2	1
6	___ of 4	4	3	2	1
7	___ of 4	4	3	2	1
8	___ of 4	4	3	2	1
9	___ of 4	4	3	2	1
10	___ of 8	7–8	5–6	3–4	2 or fewer
11	___ of 8	7–8	5–6	3–4	2 or fewer
12	___ of 4	4	3	2	1
13	___ of 4	4	3	2	1
Mid-Test	___ of 16	15–16	13–14	11–12	10 or fewer
Final Test	___ of 24	22–24	20–21	16–19	15 or fewer

Record your test score in the Your Score column. See where your score falls in the Performance columns. Your score is based on the total number of required responses. If your score is fair or needs improvement, review the chapter material.

Spectrum Mathematics
Grade 3

Answer Key

Grade 3 Answers

Chapter 1

Pretest, page 1
1. 14
2. 50
3. 34
4. 66

Lesson 1.1, page 2
1. 6
2. 9
3. 15

Lesson 1.2, page 3
1. 4
2. 3
3. 12

Lesson 1.3, page 4
1. 48
2. 45
3. 97

Lesson 1.4, page 5
1. 53
2. 56
3. 77

Lesson 1.5, page 6
1. 44
2. 36
3. 80

Lesson 1.6, page 7
1. 16
2. 46
3. 28

Lesson 1.7, page 8
1. 67
2. 86
3. 99

Lesson 1.8, page 9
1. 87
2. 39
3. 80

Posttest, page 10
1. 35
2. 43
3. 54
4. 46

Chapter 2

Pretest, page 11
1. 1,000 + 80 + 4
2. Mr. Hong; 6,000
3. >
4. Mr. Perez; 120,000

Lesson 2.1, page 12
1. 30
2. 200
3. 400 + 30 + 2; 200 + 80 + 4

Lesson 2.2, page 13
1. 900
2. 4
3. 20,000 + 5,000 + 40

Lesson 2.3, page 14
1. 8,000
2. 0
3. 200,000 + 70,000 + 200 + 10

Lesson 2.4, page 15
1. Reggie; <
2. Amy
3. Tamara

Lesson 2.5, page 16
1. 70
2. 400
3. 6,000

Posttest, page 17
1. 300 + 40 + 5
2. 40,000
3. >
4. 350; 290

Chapter 3

Pretest, page 18
1. 132
2. 502
3. 346
4. 273 − 186 = 87 or 273 − 87 = 186

Lesson 3.1, page 19
1. $36
2. $55
3. $91

Spectrum Mathematics
Grade 3

Answer Key

Grade 3 Answers

Lesson 3.2, page 20
1. 105
2. 83
3. 67

Lesson 3.3, page 21
1. 439
2. 613
3. 1,052

Lesson 3.4, page 22
1. 130
2. 244
3. 469

Lesson 3.5, page 23
1. $592 − $380 = $212 or $592 − $212 = $380
2. $302 − $134 = $168 or $302 − $168 = $134
3. $320 − $165 = $155; No. The answer is $330.

Lesson 3.6, page 24
1. $492 + $103 = $595
2. $136 + $72 = $208
3. $462 − $138 = $324; $324 + $138 = $462; No. The price should be $324.

Posttest, page 25
1. 87
2. 711
3. 243
4. 337 + 75 = 412

Chapter 4

Pretest, page 26
1. 33
2. 505
3. 447
4. 100

Lesson 4.1, page 27
1. 63
2. 88
3. 85; 103

Lesson 4.2, page 28
1. 1,733
2. 1,921
3. 2,325; 2,479

Lesson 4.3, page 29
1. 3,410
2. $5,724
3. $8,116

Lesson 4.4, page 30
1. 2,294
2. 1,014
3. 6,739

Lesson 4.5, page 31
1. 110
2. 1,600
3. $3,000

Lesson 4.6, page 32
1. 40
2. 290
3. 1,800

Posttest, page 33
1. 66
2. 833
3. 32
4. 200

Chapter 5

Pretest, page 34
1. 5 + 5 + 5 = 15
2. 45
3. 126
4. 108

Lesson 5.1, page 35
1. 5 + 5 = 10
2. 3 + 3 + 3 = 9
3. 6 × 3; 18

Lesson 5.2, page 36
1. Emilio
2. 9
3. 36

Lesson 5.3, page 37
1. 24
2. 35
3. 72

Lesson 5.4, page 38
1. $84
2. $168
3. $255

Lesson 5.5, page 39
1. 56
2. 138
3. 148

Grade 3 Answers

Posttest, page 40
1. $5 + $5 + $5 + $5 = $20
2. $24
3. $46
4. $85

Chapter 6

Pretest, page 41
1. 28; 4
2. 7
3. 5
4. 3

Lesson 6.1, page 42
1. 4; 8; 2
2. 20; 5
3. 6

Lesson 6.2, page 43
1. 3
2. 7
3. 8

Lesson 6.3, page 44
1. 6
2. 5
3. 9

Lesson 6.4, page 45
1. 4
2. 6
3. 5

Lesson 6.5, page 46
1. 8
2. 144
3. 6

Posttest, page 47
1. 18; 3
2. 9
3. 5
4. 9

Mid-Test

page 48
1. 54
2. 74
3. <
4. 96

page 49
1. 6,000 + 700 + 50 + 3
2. 6,800
3. 5,364
4. 9,171

page 50
1. 27
2. 48
3. 128
4. 85

page 51
1. 8
2. 6
3. 7
4. 9

Chapter 7

Pretest, page 52
1.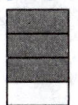
2.
3. >
4.

Lesson 7.1, page 53
1.
2.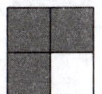
3.

Grade 3 Answers

Lesson 7.2, page 54
1. ▲ △
2. ■■□□
   ■□□□
3. $\frac{4}{10}$

Lesson 7.3, page 55
1. (shaded squares)
2. >; Lourdes
3. <; =

Posttest, page 56
1. (shaded squares)
2. (shaded rectangle)
3. =
4. Answers may vary. ■■■□
   ■■□□

Chapter 8

Pretest, page 57
1. 3
2. 12
3. 5 pounds
4. 28

Lesson 8.1, page 58
1. 3
2. 2
3. 6

Lesson 8.2, page 59
1. 7
2. 3
3. 108

Lesson 8.3, page 60
1. 3
2. 7
3. 8

Lesson 8.4, page 61
1. 34 ounces
2. 2 pounds
3. ounces

Lesson 8.5, page 62
1. 20
2. 27
3.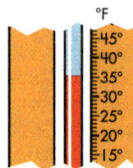

Posttest, page 63
1. 2
2. 80
3. 12 pounds
4.

Chapter 9

Pretest, page 64
1. 2
2. 1,000
3. kilograms
4. 32; 90

Lesson 9.1, page 65
1. 6
2. 4
3. 200

Lesson 9.2, page 66
1. 3
2. 6,000
3. 5,273 milliliters

Lesson 9.3, page 67
1. milligrams
2. 5 kilograms
3. 4,000

Lesson 9.4, page 68
1. 24; 75
2. 30; 86
3. Sunday

Grade 3 Answers

Posttest, page 69
1. 3 meters
2. 2,000
3. kilograms
4. 13; 55

Chapter 10

Pretest, page 70
1. 3; 78
2. $4.77
3. $10.91
4. $2.35

Pretest, page 71
1. 15; 10
2.
3. 110
4. 12

Lesson 10.1, page 72
1. 30; 6
2. 50; 5
3. 5; 95

Lesson 10.2, page 73
1. $10.67
2. $1.32
3. 90¢

Lesson 10.3, page 74
1. 82¢ or $0.82
2. $1.61
3. $4.73

Lesson 10.4, page 75
1. $1.29
2. 45¢
3. $1.13

Lesson 10.5, page 76
1. 50; 7
2. 12; 30
3. 8; 30

Lesson 10.6, page 77
1. 12
2. 5
3. 195

Posttest, page 78
1. 2; 98
2. $8.78
3. $9.70
4. $2.63

Posttest, page 79
1. 50; 6
2.
3. 7
4. 132

Chapter 11

Pretest, page 80
1. 6
2. 10
3. $\frac{1}{2}$
4. unlikely

Pretest, page 81
1. 3
2. July
3. 11
4. likely

Lesson 11.1, page 82
1. roller coaster
2. 11
3. 10

Lesson 11.2, page 83
1. Penelope
2. 12
3. 8

Lesson 11.3, page 84
1. 5
2. 65
3. 4

Lesson 11.4, page 85
1. equally likely
2. impossible
3. unlikely

Grade 3 Answers

Posttest, page 86
1. 4
2. fall
3. $\frac{1}{5}$
4. likely

Posttest, page 87
1. 10
2. 4
3. 48
4. equally likely

Chapter 12

Pretest, page 88
1. cone; solid
2. not congruent
3. symmetrical;
4. line

Lesson 12.1, page 89
1.
2. 3
3. 1

Lesson 12.2, page 90
1. 4
2. 0
3. 0
4. 8

Lesson 12.3, page 91
1. solid
2. plane
3.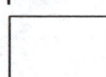

Lesson 12.4, page 92
1. not congruent
2. congruent
3.

Lesson 12.5, page 93
1. yes
2. no
3. symmetrical;
4. no

Lesson 12.6, page 94
1. line segment;
2. ray; $\vec{RS}$
3. X

Posttest, page 95
1. square; plane
2. congruent
3. yes
4.

Chapter 13

Pretest, page 96
1. 18; 14; 10
2. 5
3. 2; 4; 2; 4; 2
4.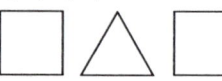

Lesson 13.1, page 97
1.
2.
3.

Lesson 13.2, page 98
1. 5; 4; 3; 2; 1
2. 1; 3; 5; 7; 9
3. 1; 2; 4; 8; 16

Lesson 13.3, page 99
1. 7; 9; 11
2. 7; 4; 1
3. 19; 23; 27

Spectrum Mathematics
Grade 3

Answer Key

116

Grade 3 Answers

Lesson 13.4, page 100
1.
2.
3.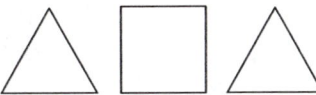

Lesson 13.5, page 101
1. 4
2. 6
3. 3

Posttest, page 102
1. 39; 41; 43
2. 4
3. 10; 9; 7; 4; 0
4.

Final Test

page 103
1.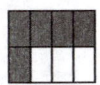
2.
3. >
4. 2

page 104
1. 3 pounds
2. 1,000
3. 0; 32
4. 12

page 105
1.
2. 135
3. 8; 99
4. 9.75; 8.99; 0.76

page 106
1. cat
2. 30
3. unlikely
4. 132

page 107
1. 6
2. solid
3. congruent
4. not symmetrical

page 108
1. 2; 4; 6; 8; 10
2. 12; 14; 16
3. 3
4.

Notes

Notes